R. J. DeCristoforo

the **Jigs & Fixtures Bible**

tips, tricks and techniques for better woodworking

POPULAR WOODWORKING BOOKS

CINCINNATI, OHIO

www.popularwoodworking.com

DEDICATION

To Mary, David & Rose Ann, R. Jay &
Lynne, and Cher Skoubo

Visit our Web site at www.popularwoodworking.com for information and more resources for woodworkers.

Other fine Popular Woodworking Books are available from your local bookstore or direct from the publisher.

09 08 07 06 05   15 14 13 12 11

Library of Congress Cataloging-in-Publication Data

DeCristoforo, R.J.
     The jigs & fixtures bible : tips, tricks and techniques for better woodworking / R.J. DeCristoforo.
          p. cm.
     ISBN 1-55870-563-5 (alk. paper)
     1. Woodworking tools–Design and construction. 2. Woodwork–Equipment and supplies–Design and construction. 3. Jigs and fixtures–Design and construction. I. Title: Jigs and fixtures bible. II. Title.

TT186 .D4273 2001
684'.08–dc21   00-065829

Editor: Daniel T. DeCristoforo
Associate Editor: Jennifer Churchill
Content Editor: Michael Berger
Designer: Brian Roeth
Layout Artist: Donna Cozatchy
Production Coordinator: Sara Dumford
Photographs and illustrations: R.J. DeCristoforo
Additional photographs: Jim Stack
Tricks of the Trade illustrations: Graham Blackburn

F·W PUBLICATIONS, INC.

Photographs used on page 4 and pages 6–13 are courtesy of the R.J. and Mary DeCristoforo family archives.

The following articles are reprinted with permission:

"Tools That Changed My Shop Forever," *Popular Woodworking* magazine, April 2000 © R.J. DeCristoforo

"Joinery," *Popular Woodworking* magazine, July 1995 © R.J. DeCristoforo

"Notched Table Saw Jigs," *Popular Woodworking* magazine, May 1996 © R.J. DeCristoforo

"Circles Without a Band Saw," *Popular Woodworking* magazine, February 2000 © R.J. DeCristoforo

"Jointers: The Forgotten Power Tool," *Popular Woodworking* magazine, March 1998 © R.J. DeCristoforo

"Jointing With Accuracy," *Popular Woodworking* magazine, November 1998 © R.J. DeCristoforo

"Put the Mortiser to Work," *Popular Woodworking* magazine, March 1996 © R.J. DeCristoforo

"Know Your Band Saw," *Popular Woodworking* magazine, July 1997 © R.J. DeCristoforo

"Band Saw Master Jig," excerpted from *The Ultimate Woodshop Jig Book*, 1999 © R.J. DeCristoforo; also published in *Popular Woodworking* magazine, July 1999

"So You Say You Don't Have a Lathe," *Popular Woodworking* magazine, March 1995 © R.J. DeCristoforo

"Mistakes of the Hand and Mind," *Popular Woodworking* magazine, September 1995 © R.J. DeCristoforo

"Making Sense of Router Bits," *Popular Woodworking* magazine, May 1995 © R.J. DeCristoforo

"Oscillating Spindle Sanders," *Popular Woodworking* magazine, January 1997 © R.J. DeCristoforo

"Miter Saw Workstation," *Popular Woodworking* magazine, September 1998 © R.J. DeCristoforo

"Master Table Saw Jig," *Popular Woodworking* magazine, September 1997 © R.J. DeCristoforo

"Maintain Your Handsaws Like a Pro," *Popular Woodworking* magazine, September 1996 © R.J. DeCristoforo

"The Moulding Cutterhead," *Popular Woodworking* magazine, May 1999 © R.J. DeCristoforo

"It's All in the Box," *Popular Woodworking* magazine, January 1999 © R.J. DeCristoforo

"The Power Curve Cutters," *Popular Woodworking* magazine, November 1995 © R.J. DeCristoforo

"A Plane Miracle," *Popular Woodworking* magazine, January 1998 © R.J. DeCristoforo

"Make Miter Joints That Have Teeth," *Popular Woodworking* magazine, July 1998 © R.J. DeCristoforo

"Another Way to Recycle," *Popular Woodworking* magazine, May 1997 © R.J. DeCristoforo

ACKNOWLEDGEMENTS

Mary A. DeCristoforo contributed significantly to this book. She helped me locate photographs and illustrations in my father's files and provided several photos from her personal collection. Mary also did fact-checking and helped edit the biographical material. Cher Skoubo, my significant other, offered constant encouragement and support. She gave freely of her time, including accompanying me on a 10-day trip to my father's California office where she assisted with retrieving and cataloging data and photographs. She also reviewed and edited my manuscripts. The editors and consultants at F&W Publications, particularly Mike Berger and Jennifer Churchill, provided essential logistical support and were very understanding about my need to attend to family matters related to my father's passing during the time I worked on this book.

— *Daniel DeCristoforo, Editor*

METRIC CONVERSION CHART

TO CONVERT	TO	MULTIPLY BY
Inches	Centimeters	2.54
Centimeters	Inches	0.4
Feet	Centimeters	30.5
Centimeters	Feet	0.03
Yards	Meters	0.9
Meters	Yards	1.1
Sq. Inches	Sq. Centimeters	6.45
Sq. Centimeters	Sq. Inches	0.16
Sq. Feet	Sq. Meters	0.09
Sq. Meters	Sq. Feet	10.8
Sq. Yards	Sq. Meters	0.8
Sq. Meters	Sq. Yards	1.2
Pounds	Kilograms	0.45
Kilograms	Pounds	2.2
Ounces	Grams	28.4
Grams	Ounces	0.04

ABOUT THE EDITOR

Daniel DeCristoforo is a freelance writer and the son of R.J. DeCristoforo. He was born in the Bronx, New York City, and raised in Palo Alto and Los Altos Hills, California. Following a tour of duty in the United States Navy during the Vietnam conflict, he returned to college and graduated from the University of California at Santa Cruz with a master's degree in geology. After 18 years in the oil and gas industry, where he worked as an exploration geologist for the Amoco Production Company and Sage Energy Company and as an independent consultant, Daniel turned his hobby of writing short stories into a full-time career. He writes a feature article and monthly column for the *LoDo & Downtown Denver News*, feature articles for *Builder/Architect* magazine and advertorial copy for *Buy Colorado* and the *Rocky Mountain News* Business and Industry section. He has written and edited brochures, Web site copy and other promotional materials for Microsoft's Denver Sidewalk, Mountain High Yogurt, the Colorado Ski Museum, Rocky Mountain Public Broadcasting and many others. Daniel lives in Denver with Cher Skoubo, a graphic artist and Webmaster working in television. The couple collaborate frequently on Web site copy and print media for advertising and marketing.

R.J. (Cris) DeCristoforo, "the Dean of Home Workshop Writers," was born in the Bronx, New York City, on April 28, 1918. He married Mary Ferrari in 1942, following a three-year courtship. He died on January 18, 2000, and is survived by his wife, Mary, and three sons — Daniel, David and R. Jay.

Cris graduated from Roosevelt High School in 1936. During WWII, after being classified 4F because of rheumatic fever, he served as foreman in charge of fabricating wingtips and ailerons for P-47 fighter planes at Republic Aviation, Farmingdale, Long Island, from 1942 to 1947. After leaving Republic, he freelanced in the home crafts field and was a contributing editor to *Popular Science*.

In 1951, Cris joined Magna Engineering in Menlo Park, California, where he wrote *Power Tool Woodworking for Everyone* and served as editorial director for promotional materials until 1956 when he returned to full-time freelance writing. Steve Shanesy, editor and publisher of *Popular Woodworking*, referred to Cris as "arguably woodworking's greatest educator" because of his "genius for explaining complex processes in clear, simple prose."

Cris was a regular contributor to a host of woodworking magazines, including *Popular Science*, *Mechanix Illustrated*, *Science and Mechanics*, *Workbench*, *Fine Woodworking* and *Better Homes and Gardens*. His feature column, *Cris Cuts*, appeared in *Popular Woodworking* through April 2000.

Cris's book titles include *DeCristoforo's House Building Illustrated*, *Woodworking Techniques: Joints and Their Application*, *Power Tool Woodworking for Everyone*, *The Complete Book of Stationary Power Tool Techniques*, *The Magic of Your Radial Arm Saw* and *Jigs, Fixtures, and Shop Accessories*.

During the 1970s, Cris served as president of the National Association of Home Woodworkers and contributed regularly to its newsletter. Men of Achievement in Cambridge, England, honored him for Distinguished Achievement in 1973. Cris was listed in Marquis's *Who's Who in the West* in 1976 and 1977. In October 1999, he was inducted into *Wood* magazine's Woodworking Hall of Fame for his collective achievements.

Here is Cris at work. His "roll-away workbench" featured a built-in table saw.

table *of* CONTENTS

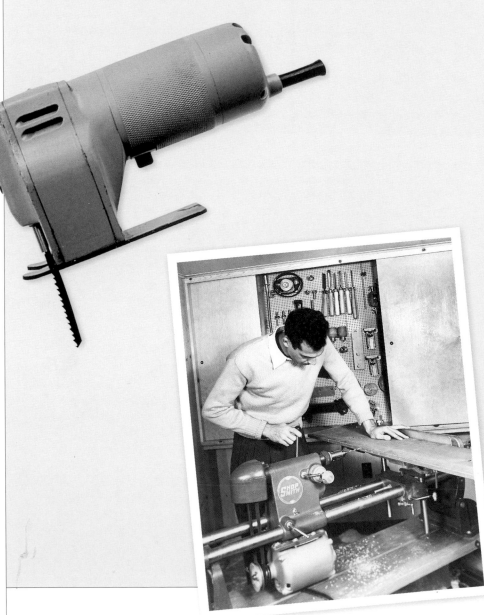

introduction

BY DANIEL T. DECRISTOFORO

Mary shows off the dining room ensemble in the Loyola Corners house. The project was a story for *Popular Science* magazine.

My father, R.J. (Cris) De-Cristoforo, began writing Cris Cuts columns for *Popular Woodworking* magazine in 1993. Cris continued to create new applications for his tools and invent more accurate and safer ways of working until the end of his life. Thus, rather than representing a rehash of old material, the columns presented here offer innovations, refinements and a fresh look at woodworking methods and techniques based on nearly 58 years of experience.

Cris periodically built new versions of his master table saw jig to extend its usefulness. Each model incorporated more sophisticated hardware. The jig was already fairly elaborate when it was first presented in the January 1994 issue of *Popular Woodworking*. By September 1997, Cris had added a more professional fence, tapering and notching jigs, and a more versatile tenoning attachment, and wrote the column that appears in this book.

Craftsmen will appreciate that the master table saw jig is a sliding table that moves with the work, eliminating the friction experienced when the work is in direct contact with the saw's table. The master table saw jig allows one to cut precise miters, and grooves in miters to hold splines and feathers. Dadoes and tenons are easily accomplished, and operations like coving and perimeter cutting to form bowls and circles become routine. With the jig, cuts on small stock, such as wedges, can be done easily and safely.

An associate of mine once remarked, though not about woodworking, that I had gotten the most out of the tools I had to work with. I considered his remark the highest of compliments. There is something immensely satisfying about extending the range of your tools — whether it's a computer, table saw, handsaw or electric drill. Cris once wrote a column about how to stock a shop with tools for under $1,000. Inflation has eroded the buying power of that budget, but Cris could still write a new version of that same article today, because he always found a way to use the tools on hand to get the job done. If you'll forgive a buzz phrase, he always worked "outside the envelope."

Why limit yourself to simple ripping and crosscutting on the table saw when the tool can do a reasonable imitation of a lathe in certain applications? In Cris's capable hands, the portable router becomes a mill shop for making mouldings, raised panel doors, decorative edges and a variety of joints. Use your band saw to cut all the curves you wish, but know that you can also split cylinders, cut accurate circles, resaw thick stock and crosscut round stock. When properly aligned, the jointer can form rabbets, tapers, chamfers, bevels, and stub and integral round tenons. The jointer also works as a plane, shapes table legs and makes recess cuts.

Readers will find a good deal of useful information in these pages about how to care for and align tools. Knowing how to sharpen your tools means that not only can you stay put in your shop, but you'll achieve cleaner and more accurate cuts that require less finishing. By working carefully, you can sharpen the knives of your jointer as well as sharpen, joint and set the teeth on handsaws. This kind of attention to detail may not be immediately obvious when a project is viewed casually, but will always show in the underlying quality of the piece and its permanence.

In a similar way, understanding how a tree grows (that the pores of the outer wood are more open than those of the older wood at the center) explains variations in the expansion and contraction of milled lumber. With this awareness in mind, you can select dense wood to join with dense, and porous wood to join with porous, meaning the project is less affected by changes in humidity. Paying attention to the alignment of wood grain helps you decide how to treat your joints: where, and where not, to apply glue and when to glue dowels in place or use them simply for alignment.

Cris pointed out in the introduction to his book on joinery that there is more to a woodworking project than meets the eye. "What is not visible or tangible bears on the quality and permanence of the project," he wrote. "Technique is more important than the materials used, and the level of intimacy one has with both tools and materials affects both the enjoyment of the process and the end result."

My father invariably stressed the importance of safety when working with tools. His primary admonition, which focuses on producing high-quality work as well as safety, was that craftsmen take care not to force the work: "Never become complacent or lose your respect for the tool." Throughout his career, Cris maintained that he was a little bit afraid of power tools, and he kept all his fingers intact despite countless hours of shop work.

"Take care to place your hands properly, keeping them out of the danger zone, and guide the work deliberately and slowly, letting the cutting edge do the work. Take your time, set everything up properly, make sure the work is held in place securely, and you will end up with a well crafted piece safely produced." If you find you're having to force things, it's a signal to recheck your setup or rethink your approach. The cutting should always feed smoothly.

The Jigs & Fixtures Bible offers novices a convenient way to learn from one of the masters, while more experienced hands will appreciate this book as an invaluable reference for brushing up on skills and techniques that may have grown rusty. Hopefully, all will find a way to use this material as a springboard to greater creativity.

Who says toys are just for kids? Cris "powers" the No-Gas Car.

R.J. DeCristoforo,
The Dean of Home Workshop Writers

REFLECTIONS ON DAD
BY DANIEL T. DECRISTOFORO

Cris relaxes in his New York apartment. The shelves were part of his first built-in wall unit.

During breaks from shop work and writing, my dad (known by his readers as "Cris") drew elegant freehand figure studies and sculpted, everything from an adaptation of *The Thinker* to a series of lifelike dinosaurs. We rarely bought anything made from wood, because Dad would say, "We can make one better than that, easy," as if that were the natural order of things. Dad had an impressive array of talents. He could have earned his living as a draftsman, photographer, writer or poet, cabinet-maker, carpenter, possibly even a fine artist.

He was a one-man team turning out 42 books and thousands of how-to articles over the course of a 50-year career as a writer and woodworker. Dad came up with the ideas, conceived the projects, designed and built the jigs needed to execute them, shot and developed the photographs, created the technical drawings and illustrations and wrote the text (including captions). Editor Burt Murphy referred to Dad as "the Dean of Home Workshop Writers."

Our Los Altos Hills, California, home brims with examples of his artistry and craftsmanship. The dish and spice cabinets in the kitchen, the built-in dining room ensemble and bar, guest coat closet, antique bookcases, spiral mobiles he called "whorl-winds," the redwood-paneled living room and matching framed windows, the hanging lamp above the brick hearth he laid himself. Now that I think of it, I don't believe there's a store-bought lamp in the entire house.

He built his-and-hers writers' studios. His studio was attached to the woodshop. With my mother and brothers, I helped him lay the Arizona-slate floor — a backbreaking job. He added a fully equipped darkroom and half-bath. Both studios were incorporated into *DeCristoforo's House Building Illustrated*. Dad converted the garage into a workshop lined with tool cabinets. Each tool, clamp, drill bit and saw blade was neatly stored in its own tray or slot.

Projects outdoors included planter boxes, Mission-style benches and tables, redwood garden shrines, a rock garden, concrete sculptures and decorative plaques, a storage shed for tools, a brick fountain and reflecting pool, and a deck above the patio overlooking the valley oaks that shade our creek. Yet, he still found time to cultivate a large vegetable garden. He canned and preserved fruits and vegetables sufficient for our own family and to share as gifts.

He bought our rustic ranch house in 1956, unfinished, set on three untamed acres, amidst apricot and walnut orchards. The multilist brochure may well have read, "needs work, unlimited potential." My cousin Joey once said to him, "Cris, you have enough projects here for a lifetime." Joey was right — more than a lifetime, as it turned out. Dad recognized, in the shell of a home, a universe of possibilities.

Several years ago, a successful contractor in Santa Barbara, California, who was a friend of my traveling companion, asked if I was related to R.J. DeCristoforo. When I answered, "Yes, he's my father," he brightened, smiled and said, "Wow, he's Mr. Table Saw; I have several of his books. His jigs are amazing."

Indeed, they are amazing. He devised many jigs and fixtures that help make woodworking easier, safer, more accurate, and that expand a power tool's usefulness beyond the manufacturer's specifications. He did this not just for the table saw, but for the band saw, radial-arm saw, drill press, lathe, router, shaper and other tools.

I delight in finding Dad's work in bookstores, especially when I can show off for friends. I'll thrust two or three volumes into their hands and say, "Here, my dad wrote these." Last year, while he was hospitalized, I made certain each of the nurses and doctors understood who they were treating: "Do you know who this is? He's the author of 42 books."

My father devoted his life to writing, consulting and teaching, helping thousands of home craftsmen create better, more imaginative work. I've always admired his quiet self-assurance. His method was to learn as much as he could about a subject, then find a better, safer, more creative way of doing it.

Dad wrote simply and directly with the authority of someone who knows what he's talking about. He was self-taught — both a great teacher and an excellent student, and completely comfortable in either role. His seemingly inexhaustible reservoir of ideas expressed itself early. In the midst of World War II, while working as a department foreman for Republic Aviation on Long Island, he was already finding creative solutions to problems and churning out projects.

Alarmed by the huge number of rivets being swept up and discarded after each shift, he devised a Rube Goldberg contraption of chutes and funnels powered by an electric drill to sort rivets. The story — a photograph and one page of copy — was purchased by *Popular Mechanics*. Dad was paid $10 for his efforts, but, more importantly, his name appeared in a how-to magazine for the first time.

Republic Aviation manufactured P-47s — new, high-powered, all-metal fighter planes — about which Dad wrote a patriotic poem called "Vengeance With Wings." "Oh, say can you feel it, the thrill that it brings? The P-47, vengeance with wings!" Published in the Republic Aviation newsletter, "Vengeance With Wings" was not his first literary effort. "Dreams," an earlier poem, was published in the *1939 Anthology of Verse*.

A 10- to 12-hour night shift and 3-hour round-trip commute between the Bronx and Republic Aviation (often in heavy Long Island fog) didn't stop Dad from writing stories and poems en route. His car-pool buddies and friends, Charlie and Joe Santarella, were enlisted as photographers for his how-to stories. Toward the end of the war, surplus materials became readily available, and Dad stocked up on aluminum, rivets and other discards for craft projects.

One of the first projects to come out of his 8' × 10' basement workshop was an heirloom clock whose small motor he synchronized with a music-box movement so that the music sounded the hour. Dad worked with hand tools and power tools that he fashioned himself. He built a lathe, powered by a motor salvaged from a coffee grinder. The first of the many power-tool improvisations for which he became famous was a table that converted a portable magnetic jigsaw into a stationary power tool. The story "Put Your Jigsaw to Work" merited a four-page spread in *Popular Mechanics*.

Some of my father's projects remain as much a part of me as the alphabet and basic arithmetic. We still use his ornamental jewelry box made of aluminum with the chamfered maple top

R.J. "Cris" DeCristoforo.

and green-felt base. *Popular Science* ran the story. My mother tells of many aluminum nut bowls and serving trays given away as gifts after the stories were published.

Years later, after we'd moved to California, Dad customized the kitchen cabinets in our first Los Altos Hills home (Loyola Corners) with built-in lazy Susans, spice racks, compartmentalized utensil drawers, towel racks, and utility shelves; truly there was a place for everything and everything had its place.

The real treasure in the Loyola Corners house was a built-in dining room unit complete with a foldout table, touch-latch doors, bar and liquor cabinet, china cabinet and utensil drawer. Dad moved a Shopsmith into the house during construction. The finished unit was faced with golden ash that matched the table and, when extended, the table revealed an illuminated panel on top of which sat an intriguing piece of gnarled, chocolate-colored driftwood, in striking contrast to the golden ash.

When we moved from Loyola Corners, it was the customized kitchen cabinets and the dining room wall unit that had sold the house. Dad bought our family home, a ranch house on Natoma Road, and installed a new version of the built-in dining room. It, too, had a pulldown table, a bar and

Deer frequently feed by the porch outside Mary's studio in Los Altos Hills.

plenty of slots and compartments, but for me, the Loyola Corners built-in was irreplaceable. One drawback to built-ins: You can't take them with you.

The progenitor of the Loyola Corners dining unit was a writing table and work area for my mother in our New York apartment, complete with window-frame bookcases, an upholstered window seat and storage chest and foldaway desk. Dad's window-frame article featured a photo of Mom seated at her pulldown desk in front of a new Remington typewriter, a gift from Dad.

Mother, also a writer, frequently sold to newspapers, women's magazines and the confession market when she wasn't helping Dad with his writing or modeling with his projects. Dad typed with two fingers and was not the best grammarian or speller, but he got capable, professional help from Mom, who was adept at all three — typing, spelling and grammar.

Determined to make a career of how-to writing, Dad drove a delivery truck for Riviera Ravioli twice a week to supplement his meager income. Fortunately, editors were beginning to notice his contributions. Virg Angerman, publisher of *Science and Mechanics* in Chicago, offered encouragement and began sending assignments.

The first time he visited Dad,

Angerman requested a story on metal etching and gave Dad a generous advance for a comprehensive series of articles on leathercraft. Undaunted by the fact that he knew little or nothing of either subject, Dad experimented with both crafts and read as much as he could.

He fashioned tools out of clock gears, nails and wooden dowels, and devised embossing jigs. These he used to make a bowling bag, a hunter's cap, a lady's belt and matching shoulder bag, an elaborately tooled gun belt and holster reflecting his fascination with the West, a lampshade decorated with flowers, and a wallet for Angerman. Virg was impressed enough to call and congratulate Dad on his unique designs and innovative tools. The gun belt and holster, still on display in Dad's studio, is another of my favorites.

Angerman put Dad on the masthead of *Science and Mechanics* as "Contributing Editor" and eventually supplied him with a versatile new power tool, the Shopsmith. Today we might say flex tool; Angerman called it a shop-in-a-toolbox. Shopsmiths function as table saw, vertical and horizontal drill press, lathe, band saw and disc-and-drum sander, and they convert quickly and easily from one mode to another.

Shopsmith was the perfect tool for home craftsmen with space constraints or a limited budget. Dad's first Shopsmith projects were bowls and lamp bases turned on the lathe, because only a small amount of wood was required and, noise being a consideration in our apartment building, the lathe was relatively quiet.

Popular Science, Mechanix Illustrated, Popular Mechanics and *Workbench* accepted and solicited Dad's work with increasing frequency. As an expression of gratitude to Magna Engineering for providing a Shopsmith, Dad made certain its logo appeared prominently in

photographs. When Robert L. Chambers, president of Magna Engineering, who was scouring how-to magazines looking for someone to write a book on the Shopsmith, came to New York, a meeting with Dad was on his itinerary.

Suddenly, Dad had two terrific opportunities. Virg Angerman wanted him in Chicago to head up the Home Workshop Division as editor, and Bob Chambers wanted him to become Magna Engineering's editorial director and write the Shopsmith book in California. After a series of family pow-wows during which, I'm told, I voted to remain in New York, the decision was made to move cross-country to what was then often referred to as the land of milk and honey.

Our first California home was a rental on Park Boulevard, across El Camino Real from Stanford University in Palo Alto. Park Boulevard was lined with magnolias and palm trees, and, although we were shortly forced to join the growing commuter culture, Magna Engineering was "just up the road" in Menlo Park. After the cramped New York apartment and tiny basement workshop, our new surroundings felt roomy and expansive.

Magna installed two Shopsmiths in our garage. We never used garages for parking or storage; they were forever

This Mission-style china cabinet was built by Cris.

"the shop." During the next few years, Dad wrote a series of Shopsmith instruction manuals, consulted with Shopsmith inventor Hans Goldschmidt on accessories to expand Shopsmith's already considerable versatility and wrote his first, and perhaps most popular, book, *Power Tool Woodworking for Everyone.* When Goldschmidt phoned, he invariably kidded: "This is the world's greatest inventor. May I speak with the world's greatest how-to writer?" *Power Tool Woodworking for Everyone* remains an essential reference and "must reading" for users of Shopsmith.

Dad's shop, where most of the projects and jigs used in the book were built, was heated by a pot-bellied stove; though never terribly cold, the weather was often quite damp and the concrete floor a poor insulator.

Shopsmith's range was demonstrated in a feature story photographed by Hollywood photographer Peter Gowland for *American Home Magazine* about how to build an authentic early-American grandfather clock. Working at night and on weekends, Dad continued producing projects and stories for *Science and Mechanics* and *Popular Science,* including a piece on built-in bookcases.

Early versions of several of Dad's jigs appeared in *Power Tool Woodworking for Everyone.* Much of his career as a freelancer was devoted to refining those jigs and developing new ones, not just for Shopsmith, but for many other power tools. Dad also evaluated tools for Stanley, Black & Decker, and Sears Roebuck, a practice begun at Magna Engineering where he tested the saw blades Disston Corporation supplied for the Shopsmith.

After he left Magna, Dad began focusing more and more of his attention on books. Many have come to be recognized as authoritative works, for example, *The Complete Book of Wood Joinery* and *DeCristoforo's Complete Book of Power Tools, Both Stationary and Portable. De-Cristoforo's House Building Illustrated* remains in print after 15 years.

Dad showed how the radial-arm saw could be almost as versatile as the Shopsmith in teaching woodworkers how to cut, among other things, tapers, compound miters, mouldings, bowls, circles, latticelike decorative pieces and table legs. He also used the tool as a router, shaper, planer and disc-and-drum sander. With his special jigs and attachments, the saw performed certain drilling operations and mimicked a lathe and a saber saw. For Dad, almost any tool became an "all-in-one."

Dad's master table saw jig (see "Master Table Saw Jig" chapter) combines a miter-gauge function with crosscutting, dadoing and tenoning capabilities. The jig's sliding table effectively eliminates creep, "that spoiler of accuracy," a common problem associated with a standard miter gauge. "The master jig's long fence provides a greater support surface than a miter gauge," he wrote. "The table and the work move together, thus eliminating the friction that is present when work directly contacts the saw's table.

"Despite the fact that power tools have accuracy and a good amount of built-in control, it is often necessary for the woodworker to invent accessories or learn techniques that enable him to precisely and safely duplicate project components with a minimum of fuss. Sometimes an idea is adopted for temporary use; more often, however, the project or idea becomes a lifetime accessory that deserves time and care when it is being constructed."

Shortly after he returned to freelancing, Dad made a trip to visit publishers and editors, including Robert Stevenson at *Popular Science,* John Sill at Popular Science Book Club, and Larry Eisenger at Fawcett. Eisenger gave him an advance for *The New Handyman's Carpentry Guide,* the first of more than a dozen softcover books he would write for Fawcett. A contact he made at DeWalt eventually led to the book on radial-arm saws. Dad wrote regularly for Al Lees at *Popular Science,* Burt Murphy of *Mechanix Illustrated* and Jay Hedden of *Workbench.*

My parents christened the years between 1965 and the mid-1980s the

A place for everything. The family's Loyola Corners kitchen cabinets were featured in *Better Homes and Gardens.*

"golden age of do-it-yourself." Craftwork and woodworking were exceedingly popular, tools sales were at an all-time high, Shopsmith units and *Power Tool Woodworking for Everyone* sold briskly, and editors regularly asked Dad for new stories and books. A series of power-tool stories for *Popular Science* became *DeCristoforo's Complete Book of Power Tools,* and Dad contributed articles to three do-it-yourself encyclopedias. Mom wrote an article about Dad for the Peninsula Living section of the *San Francisco Chronicle,* "How to Parlay Your Hobby Into a Successful Career."

By 1986, Dad had completed more than 30 books intended for the home woodworker. A revised and updated edition of *The Complete Book of Wood Joinery* was released in 1993, the same year that *Jigs, Fixtures, and Shop Accessories* appeared. In recent years, Dad limited his shop work, but he continued to produce his column, Cris Cuts, for *Popular Woodworking,* wrote *The Ultimate Woodshop Jig Book* and continued to write how-to stories. Increasingly, he returned to his fiction and poetry.

He never stopped teaching and encouraging others, myself included; and in something of a turnabout, he acted as editor and consultant on my mother's memoir *Chicken Tonight — Feathers Tomorrow.*

Who is the young man demonstrating horizontal boring on the Shopsmith 10ER?
Why it's R.J. DeCristoforo himself, using the first power tool he ever owned.

Tools That Changed My Shop Forever

The dean of home workshop writers gives you a personal look inside his shop and the tools we now take for granted.

In the late 1940s, the Shopsmith, a power tool that contributed significantly to the growth of amateur woodworking, was placed on the market. It was a multipurpose machine, a five-in-one concept that was greeted lovingly by some and with skepticism by others — the latter group being woodworkers who couldn't understand why you would want to rearrange components to change from a table saw to a drill press. They also didn't like the fact that the machine had a tilting table (instead of a tilting arbor), though most people forget that many saws of the time were built that way.

Nearly one million woodworkers have bought a Shopsmith, which gives you an assortment of power tools without taking up much more space than a couple bicycles. I admit to a degree of fondness for the machine because the introductory model, the 10ER, was my first power tool. It allowed me to work efficiently in my shop of the time, an 8' × 10' corner of an apartment basement.

Whatever I did with the tool impressed the manufacturer enough to transport me from New York to California so I could produce the Shopsmith bible, *Power Tool Woodworking for Everyone*. There have been transformations since then in the book, the tool, manufacturers and my interest in tools generally. But one factor seems perennial, the camaraderie that exists among users of multipurpose machines.

Since that first machine entered my life years ago, I've had the opportunity to use hundreds of woodworking tools. Some of them changed forever the way we work. The following is a look at the tools that earned a permanent place in my shop.

SABER SAW

Some tools achieve overnight success. The saber saw, imported from Switzerland in the 1940s, was quickly adopted by professional and amateur woodworkers, despite its $150 price. How can you not be impressed with a small, lightweight tool that can substitute for a handsaw, portable circular saw, jigsaw, band saw, coping saw and keyhole saw? With a pivot guide it can saw perfect circles, and it can form its own starting hole.

Importers soon had considerable competition from American manufacturers, which resulted in added features and lower prices. Stanley, Black & Decker, Millers Falls, Porter-Cable, Sears, Wen and others produced saber saws with about a $50 or $60 price tag. Some were as low as $30. Disston, famed for its handsaws, even produced a 5-pound saber saw that had a handle that duplicated the one on its famous D-23 handsaw.

Disston's "Dial-a-Power" drill gave woodworkers electronic variable speed. The in-line motor and handle allowed woodworkers to get their weight behind the tool (*above*). Black & Decker's first portable electric drill opened up a world of possibilities for home woodworkers (*below*).

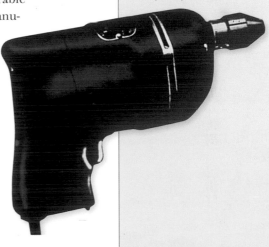

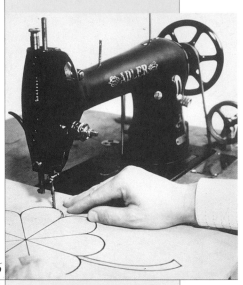

16

Early jigsaws and scroll saws shared a common ancestor, a sewing machine with a blade in place of the needle. An employee of Bosch came up with the idea. Now Bosch makes what is considered to be the premium jigsaw for professionals and serious home users.

ELECTRIC DRILL

It would be unusual to discover a shop without a portable electric drill. My first one was a monster, a ⅜" unit that was surplus from an aircraft plant that was scaling down at the end of World War II. My drill was heavy and awkward by today's standards, with a design that, with consistent use, could lead to carpal tunnel syndrome. But it served me well. I made a stand for it so I could also use it for drum sanding, grinding and buffing.

A few years later I tested the new Disston ¼", 1,800 rpm drill that looked like a paint sprayer. I thought the design made sense. Its "in-line" drive feature placed your hand directly behind the bit, and that let you drill straighter and with more muscle.

The drill's offset motor and recessed chuck gave it the slimmest profile in the business. I could sneak into tight corners and drill closer to obstructions than with other drills. And, of course, I built a stand-up base to make it more versatile.

A year or two later Disston reintroduced the drill with an important feature: electronic variable speed. A small dial set the speed anywhere between 600 and 2,000 rpms, and at any setting you had the full power of the motor. The drills were not on the market long. You might see one in a tool museum, or in my shop where I stored the prototypes.

About 20 years ago Makita changed the world of portable drills by introducing the 6010D, the first cordless tool. That first model can't compete with what's on the market today, but the concept was revolutionary.

AFFORDABLE THICKNESS PLANERS

One of my wishes was granted when I bought a thickness planer. Professionals may be too blasé to be impressed with such a machine, but I am awed at what my little one can do. Maybe that's because I remember when I used a belt sander or rotary planer in a drill press to thickness my stock. Or I had to haul it to a local lumberyard to pay someone to plane it for me.

Affordable thickness planing became feasible at home when Ryobi introduced the AP10, a 10" thickness planer. Now there are about a dozen units to choose from that can handle stock up to 13" wide and 6" thick — well within the requirements of a small home or commercial shop.

BISCUIT JOINER

I could easily compete in any survey that sought to determine who has made the most dowel joints. I've gone the gamut in dowel technology — trying to tolerate ready-made dowels that are never the size they are supposed to be,

The first jigsaw looked much like today's models, but modern tools are packed with features unheard of when the tool was introduced *(left)* (photo courtesy of Bosch). Pad sanders helped ease one of the most dreaded aspects of woodworking: finishing. This Rockwell sander was the first one R.J. DeCristoforo owned *(middle)*. An early router from the Carter company did not have the boatload of features that the modern models do, but the basic concept was still true: a spinning bit on the shaft of a motor *(right)*.

using plug cutters to custom-make dowels, commercial and homemade doweling jigs, using a drill press and so on.

Years ago I switched to a plate joiner, a portable tool that takes the drudgery out of many joinery tasks. This simple tool uses a small carbide-tipped circular saw to cut a half-oval cavity in the edges of mating components. Football-shaped biscuits are glued into the cavities formed by the tool. When the biscuits absorb the moisture in the glue, they swell and expand to fit tightly in the joint.

I've always liked the simplicity of the layout needed to use this tool. You place the mating pieces together as they will be joined and mark a line across the joint. Then you align the tool with the mark on each piece and make your plunge cuts.

The plate joiner, which was initially a European import, was for professionals at first because of its high cost. About a dozen years ago, Freud introduced the JS100 model, which was reasonably priced. Judicious shoppers could buy one for a lot less than the $270 list price. Today you can buy an outstanding tool for between $100 and $300.

SCROLL SAW

When the scroll saw was first introduced, many woodworkers were disinterested because they viewed it as something for crafts or jigsaw puzzles.

The origin of the scroll saw began centuries ago with treadle-powered machines made with wooden components. The same concept was used in sawmills that had a huge reciprocating saw blade to cut rough stock to size. The small units we now use were made possible by the advent of fine-toothed scrolling blades and compact electric motors.

My first powered scroll saw was my sister's treadle-type sewing machine that I had modified by installing a fractional horsepower motor. This happened because an employee of the Bosch Manufacturing Company thought of replacing the needle on his wife's sewing machine with a small blade. I tested and adopted the idea. Now we might smile at the concept,

but I did OK with it for quite a while.

Modern machines have eclipsed their ancestors' reputation for cutting gingerbread and become an important woodworking machine. They can handle stock up to 2" thick with the table at 90°. And it is adept at "pad sawing," which allows you to layer multiple pieces and cut them all at once.

BENCHTOP MORTISER

For most of my woodworking life I made mortises with a mortising accessory on my drill press. I've never complained about this method, but I often thought it would be nice to have a permanent mortising setup.

The new benchtop mortisers give you a quick setup for mortising, and make the operation easier. For example, the Delta unit that I recently tried out borrows from the arbor press used in metalworking. Its husky steel arbor and long handle let you convert 32 pounds of downward force into 320 pounds. The gearing allows you to make a complete cut with a 90° pull of the handle. A similar cut on a drill press would require you to turn the feed lever a full circle.

ROUTER

I've done my share of routing with hand tools, namely, Stanley planes designed for dadoing or combination machines that formed flutes, fillets and other moulding designs. While the tools strengthened my arms, I was happy to switch to an electric router — one of the wonder tools in woodworking.

The history of the router goes back to World War I, its invention generally credited to R.L. Carter, a patternmaker who designed a cutter from the worm gear of an electric barber's clipper and secured it to the shaft of an electric motor. The efficiency of the "Electric Hand Shaper" was quickly noticed and Carter found himself producing thousands of the units for sale. In the late 1920s, Stanley acquired the Carter business and produced the first "modern" router, not especially for me, of course.

There's little point to touting the virtues of the portable router because, "Is there a woodworker with a soul so dead he never to himself has said, 'I love my router'?" The mechanics of the router haven't changed but improvements continue to make it an exciting tool, especially the plunge feature.

What's next? A recent innovation is a wrench-free collet, something like the keyless chuck on a drill. I haven't had the chance to check it out, but if it eliminates having to use two wrenches in a tight area, I'll buy it.

DOVETAIL JIGS

Before the advent of dovetail jigs, you had to cut this joint by hand. Even though these jigs made the task quick, we didn't fully embrace the concept because the first jigs dictated the width of the stock you could use and spaced the tails perfectly evenly. In the early 1980s, the Leigh jig from a Canadian company changed all that. You can vary the spacing of the pins and tails on any workpiece up to 24" wide. It also cuts a wide variety of joints, even sliding dovetails. Needless to say, careful adjustment of components is required.

ELECTRIC SANDERS

When it comes to preparing wood for finishing, I'm open to anything that makes the chore easier. So when power sanders made their debut, I was a quick customer. My first unit was the Rockwell "speed bloc sander" that was later acquired and is still being produced by Porter-Cable. The unit has a high speed of 12,000 orbits per minute and works with one-quarter sheets of sandpaper.

As I mentioned, I'm addicted to speedy wood smoothing, so my shop has a special cabinet filled with portable sanders, belt sanders, detail sanders and the relatively new random-orbit tools.

One claim of these random-orbit sanders is that their high speed and tiny orbits eliminate cross-grained scratches and swirls. A counterclaim is

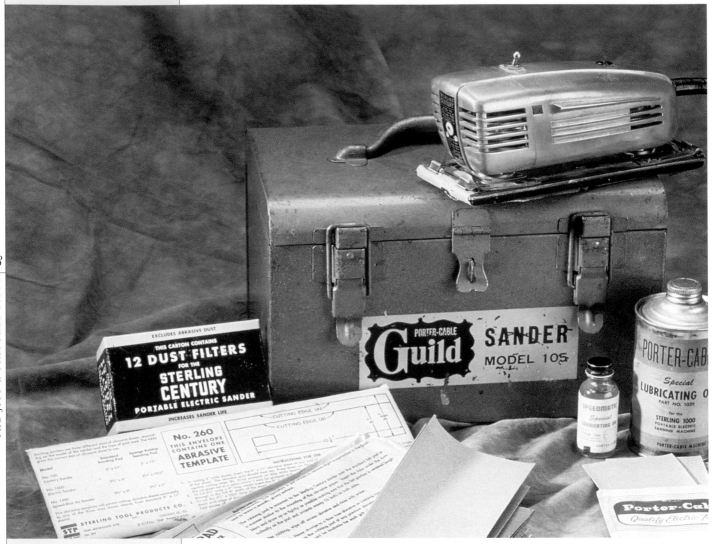

This early sander looks more like a toaster. Woodworkers didn't care what sanders looked like as long as they quickly smoothed the wood. (Photo courtesy of Porter-Cable.)

that no matter which sander you use, some hand sanding is necessary.

CARBIDE

Not all innovations come in the form of tools; some are materials, notably, tungsten carbide. My first experience with a carbide-tipped blade was with a Disston 8-tooth design that was offered as a "safety blade." Why, I don't know. All I could see was the blade thunk, thunk, thunking through a saw cut. It wasn't exciting except to construction workers who used it in portable saws to cut through house-framing members.

In the late 1970s and early 1980s, woodworking magazines inundated

readers with praises of multitoothed carbide blades. High cost was a factor, but superior performance and a life span of as much as 20 to 1 over steel blades made the price seem more reasonable. We now take carbide blades for granted.

But carbide has made a more general impact. There are few cutting tools that can't be obtained with carbide edges: dado blades, router bits, shaper cutters and blades for planers and jointers. All of these make our workshop effort easier and more professional.

What will follow? Will we get to sawing wood with laser beams?

The Basics of Table Saw Angles

Simple and compound angles are

a breeze on the table saw.

Any multisided project like the examples in drawing 1 requires a miter-gauge setting or a blade tilt. Both adjustments are required in a particular relationship when the project has sloping sides (see drawing 2).

When you think of the nitty-gritty of preparing segments for the project, you realize that the chore is accomplished with basic sawing. Accuracy is critical ... but it always is. No reason to get shaky when multiple segments are involved. Being careful when making adjustments and making test-cuts before cutting good stock is normal procedure even when making a one-time miter or bevel cut.

POLYGONS

Segments for polygons (drawing 3) are prepared with the miter gauge when the project is flat; a blade tilt is needed when the project has depth. The cut angle is the same for either design. The prevailing factor is that the angles of the saw cuts must add up to 360°.

Arriving at the correct angle is simple as shown by the example (drawing 4). Divide 360 by the number of segments the project must have to get the *joint* angle. Then divide this in half to get the *cut* angle each of the segments needs.

Determining the width of the segments can be done mathematically,

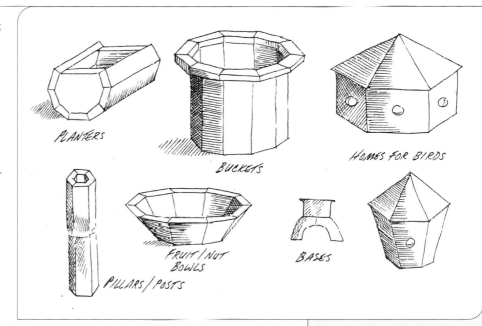

PLANTERS

BUCKETS

HOMES FOR BIRDS

FRUIT / NUT BOWLS

PILLARS / POSTS

BASES

Drawing 1.

but I use the more basic approach of using a drawing, scaled if necessary (drawing 5). The result can be increased or decreased a bit to arrive at a reasonable fraction without affecting the size of the project dramatically.

SAWING

Segments can be prepared individually, but a better procedure — one that substantially reduces the possibility of human error — is to do the beveling on a long board and then crosscut the board into necessary lengths (photos 1 and 2).

I allow myself an "out" on projects of this nature. It's easy to make the point that if you cut accurately, the segments will assemble in pristine fash-

1 Doing the beveling on a long board is the best way to produce material for the segments required for straight-sided projects.

2 Crosscut the beveled board by using a stop-block on the rip fence to gauge the length of the segments.

3 Strip-cutting to produce the segments for projects with sloping sides simplifies the procedure and saves material. Use an extension on the miter gauge that is long enough to support the parent stock.

Drawing 2.

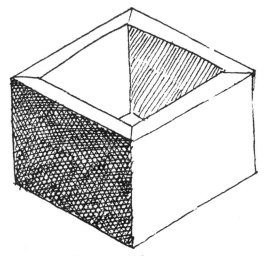

A PROJECT WITH STRAIGHT SIDES REQUIRES MITER (OR BEVEL) CUTS—
THE JOINT IS A COMPOUND ANGLE IF THE PROJECT HAS SLOPING SIDES.
THE FACT APPLIES REGARDLESS OF THE NUMBER OF SIDES IN THE PROJECT.

ion. But, for myself and "just in case," I cut all the segments but one and then do a test assembly and prepare the last segment to fit, something like the keystone in a masonry arch (drawing 6).

COMPOUND CUTS

Multisided projects with sloping sides require that segments be prepared by combining a blade tilt and a miter-gauge setting. It follows naturally to make the point that since two settings are needed (and they must have the correct relationship in terms of work slope and number of sides) that error possibility is doubled. But, again, success is achieved by making trial cuts before cutting good stock. Naturally, the blade tilt and miter-gauge settings can't be arbitrary, which is why we offer the charts (on page 23).

As with bevel sawing, the segments can be cut from individual pieces or continuously from a long board. Strip-cutting should be used whenever possible since it simplifies the procedure and saves material (photo 3). The board is inverted for alternate cuts.

When the top and bottom edges of the project must be flat, the components are beveled; the bevel angle is the same as the slope angle of the project (drawing 7).

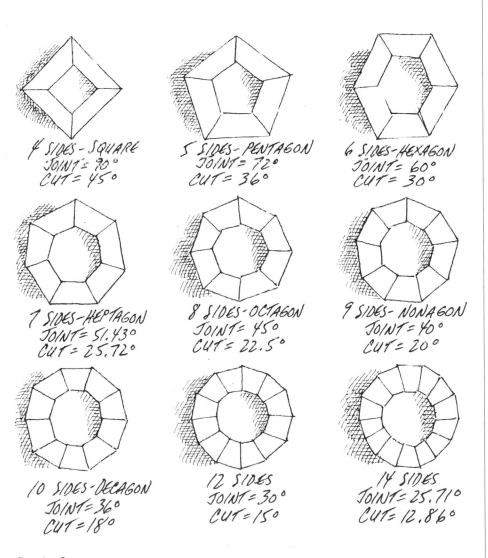

4 SIDES - SQUARE
JOINT = 90°
CUT = 45°

5 SIDES - PENTAGON
JOINT = 72°
CUT = 36°

6 SIDES - HEXAGON
JOINT = 60°
CUT = 30°

7 SIDES - HEPTAGON
JOINT = 51.43°
CUT = 25.72°

8 SIDES - OCTAGON
JOINT = 45°
CUT = 22.5°

9 SIDES - NONAGON
JOINT = 40°
CUT = 20°

10 SIDES - DECAGON
JOINT = 36°
CUT = 18°

12 SIDES
JOINT = 30°
CUT = 15°

14 SIDES
JOINT = 25.71°
CUT = 12.86°

Drawing 3.

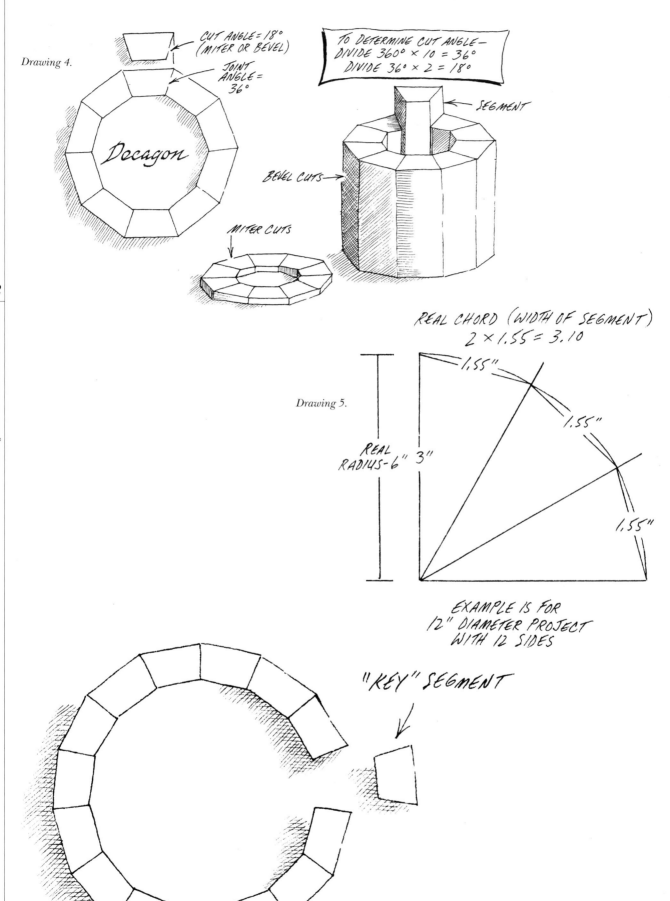

Drawing 4.

CUT ANGLE=18°
(MITER OR BEVEL)

JOINT ANGLE = 36°

TO DETERMINE CUT ANGLE—
DIVIDE 360° × 10 = 36°
DIVIDE 36° × 2 = 18°

SEGMENT

Decagon

BEVEL CUTS

MITER CUTS

REAL CHORD (WIDTH OF SEGMENT)
2 × 1.55 = 3.10

1.55"

1.55"

Drawing 5.

REAL RADIUS-6" 3"

1.55"

1.55"

EXAMPLE IS FOR
12" DIAMETER PROJECT
WITH 12 SIDES

"KEY" SEGMENT

Drawing 6.

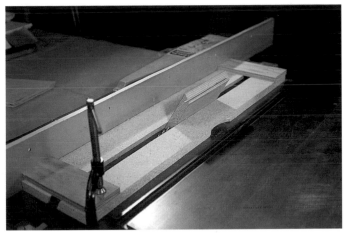

4 A simple jig makes it easy to form accurate spline grooves. Make the jig long enough so it can be clamped to the table.

5 The same jig is used for spline grooves whether you are working with compound angles or simple bevels.

REINFORCEMENTS

Splines are a good choice for adding strength to the project, and they are a help at assembly time. Making the spline grooves accurately requires the simple jig that is demonstrated in photos 4 and 5. The jig consists of parallel strips that are beveled at the same angle used on the components (drawing 8).

Drawing 7.

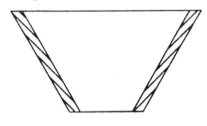

Top and bottom edges of components are beveled when they must be flat. The bevel angle is the same as the tilt (slope) of the project. Do this before making the compound angle cuts.

Drawing 8.

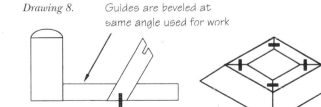

Guides are beveled at same angle used for work

Blade is square

chart one • applies when the miter gauge reads 0° in neutral position

SLOPE	4 SIDES		6 SIDES		8 SIDES	
ANGLE	BLADE	GAUGE	BLADE	GAUGE	BLADE	GAUGE
5°	$44^3/4$	5	$29^3/4$	$2^1/2$	$22^1/4$	2
10°	$44^1/4$	$9^3/4$	$29^1/4$	$5^1/2$	22	4
15°	$43^1/4$	$14^1/2$	29	$8^1/4$	$21^1/2$	6
20°	$41^3/4$	$18^3/4$	$28^1/4$	11	21	8
30°	$37^3/4$	$26^1/2$	26	16	$19^1/2$	$11^3/4$
40°	$32^1/2$	$32^3/4$	$22^3/4$	$20^1/4$	17	15
50°	27	$37^1/2$	19	$23^3/4$	$14^1/2$	$17^1/2$
60°	21	41	$14^1/2$	$26^1/2$	11	$19^3/4$

chart two • applies when the miter gauge reads 90° in neutral position

SLOPE	4 SIDES		6 SIDES		8 SIDES	
ANGLE	BLADE	GAUGE	BLADE	GAUGE	BLADE	GAUGE
5°	$44^3/4$	85	$29^3/4$	$87^1/2$	$22^1/4$	88
10°	$44^1/4$	$80^1/4$	$29^1/2$	$84^1/2$	22	86
15°	$43^1/4$	$75^1/2$	29	$81^3/4$	$21^1/2$	84
20°	$41^3/4$	$71^1/4$	$28^1/4$	79	21	82
30°	$37^3/4$	$63^1/2$	26	74	$19^1/2$	$78^1/4$
40°	$32^1/2$	$57^1/4$	$22^3/4$	$69^3/4$	17	75
50°	27	$52^1/2$	19	$66^1/4$	$14^1/2$	$72^1/2$
60°	21	49	$14^1/2$	$63^1/2$	11	$70^1/4$

Joinery

Where beauty's more than skin deep ... and knowing your material will help predict its behavior.

There's more to most woodworking projects than meets the eye. Reaction to the appearance of your finished work is subjective, a factor that eludes definition. But beyond the outward appearance, buried below the finish, lies something tangible. It greatly affects the quality and permanence of the project. These invisible details, the woodworking joints you make, demonstrate both your knowledge and your skill. There are choices made along the route to a finished work, but little room for compromise. A joint will hold, possibly forever, or it will fail. Accepting the nature of your chosen wood and working accordingly is as important as accurate cutting.

Knowledge of wood and its characteristics, even the subtle differences from one species to another, is an important ally in your campaign to make lasting joints. Start with our understanding of how a tree grows — outward from its center, each year adding a roughly concentric ring of new wood. The cells or pores of the "new" wood are more open than the center ones, so wood from that area is subject to greater shrinkage and expansion. The changes in wood, after it is sawed into boards, is natural and continuous; the dryness/dampness of the environment affects the degree of change.

To counteract varying degrees of contraction and expansion, when joining boards to form a slab, be certain to place new wood against new wood, old wood against old. It's the most that can be done to guard against uneven joints caused by humidity.

There are several points of view regarding the best methods of minimizing warpage (or cupping) when joining boards edge to edge. A common practice, with a single board, is to rip it into thirds and to rejoin the pieces after inverting the center one. Whether this will be a solution can be determined by judging the degree of warpage. If it is extreme, each of the pieces will have its own "cup" and the assembly will require considerable planing and sanding (diagram 1A). My own procedure with a "bad" board is to save it for when I need narrow strips.

Alternate boards (for a slab) are often inverted to compensate for cupping caused by shrinkage (diagram 1B). This system can result in a washboard surface that will be difficult to pin down, and it's possible that alter-

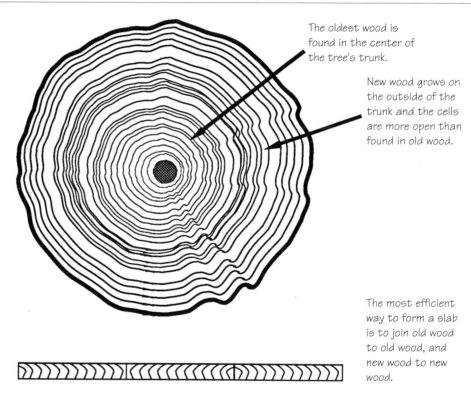

The oldest wood is found in the center of the tree's trunk.

New wood grows on the outside of the trunk and the cells are more open than found in old wood.

The most efficient way to form a slab is to join old wood to old wood, and new wood to new wood.

Typical Gluing Errors

Glue is a "fastener" so, to avoid splitting, we should avoid using it when a component needs to move. An example is a panel door with a solid-wood insert. When the panel wants to "move" but is held tightly around its entire perimeter, its only choice is to split or separate near the glue line. The frame must be solid and tight, but the insert piece should be free. Another example concerns narrow boards used at the ends of solid-wood slabs. This makes sense, but not if the boards are glued their entire length. They will remain constant in length but the width of the pieces in the slab may change, and they can split if they don't have freedom to move. The solution is simple: Use glue, or a dowel, only at the center of each of the pieces in the slab.

With end boards, you can use the same "extra" technique we mentioned for edge-to-edge joints. That is, use a plane or jointer to slightly concave the edge of the board that butts against the slab assembly. The board will continue to exert pressure after the center area is forced in with clamps.

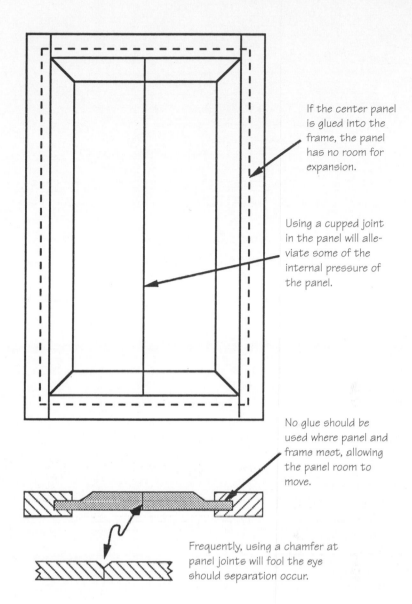

If the center panel is glued into the frame, the panel has no room for expansion.

Using a cupped joint in the panel will alleviate some of the internal pressure of the panel.

No glue should be used where panel and frame meet, allowing the panel room to move.

Frequently, using a chamfer at panel joints will fool the eye should separation occur.

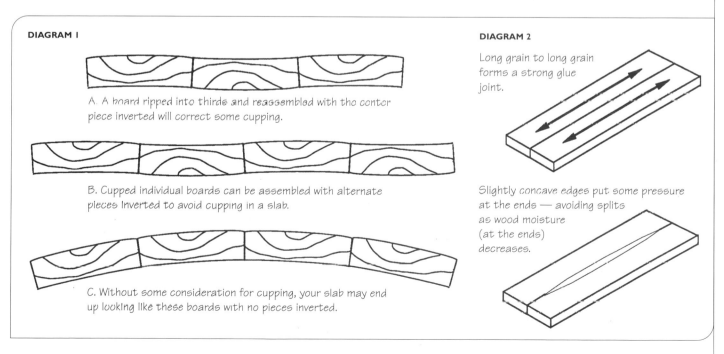

DIAGRAM 1

A. A board ripped into thirds and reassembled with the center piece inverted will correct some cupping.

B. Cupped individual boards can be assembled with alternate pieces inverted to avoid cupping in a slab.

C. Without some consideration for cupping, your slab may end up looking like these boards with no pieces inverted.

DIAGRAM 2

Long grain to long grain forms a strong glue joint.

Slightly concave edges put some pressure at the ends — avoiding splits as wood moisture (at the ends) decreases.

DIAGRAM 3

The "long grain" of the dowel runs "across" the grain of the boards causing a stable wood — unstable wood match.

DIAGRAM 4

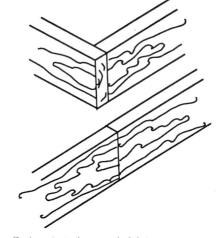

End-grain to long-grain joints and end-grain to end-grain joints have little strength and will likely fail.

DIAGRAM 5

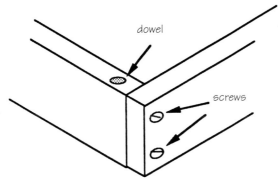

dowel

screws

Screwing into a dowel is one way to reinforce an end-grain to long-grain butt joint.

DIAGRAM 6

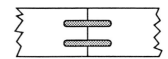

Using dowels will reinforce an end-grain to end-grain joint since dowels and the wood make long-grain contact.

nate pieces will contain a lot of sapwood. When the boards are not inverted, the assembly will form a gentle arc that requires little surface treatment and that will actually be easier to pin down (diagram 1C). Also, there is more opportunity to place the boards for compatible grain pattern.

The strongest glue joint occurs when long grain connects to long grain. Thus, the vital consideration when joining boards is the condition of the mating edges. They must be square and flat, although the extra step shown in the drawing is often included (diagram 2). The slight concave edge, which can be accomplished with a plane or on a jointer, causes a slight pressure at the end of the boards. The pressure is released as the wood gives off moisture, thus guarding against end splits. If wood breaks when joined this way it will not break in the joint. In fact, tests to break the connection prove that the glue line holds while areas around it break apart. There is evidence that dowels used to reinforce an edge-to-edge joint are unnecessary and can actually cause harm (diagram 3). For one thing, the dowel, being long grain, remains fairly stable, but the wood it enters may not. This can result in splits around the joint area. If I use dowels I rely on them only for alignment of components, so I don't glue them.

A butt joint between end grain and long grain typifies a weak glue joint that requires reinforcement (diagram 4). Even screws don't help much since the bulk of the screw will penetrate end grain. One way to add strength is to insert a dowel into the long-grain piece so the screws will have something to bite into (diagram 5).

End-grain to end-grain joints are almost a lost cause, but here, dowels can provide strength since they and the wood make long-grain contact (diagram 6).

Notched Table Saw Jigs

These jigs have the answers to simplifying your toughest cutting chores.

When you need a component that can't be sawed accurately by conventional means, such as using a miter gauge or rip fence, or one that is too small to be hand-held safely, you may discover that a simple "notched jig" offers a practical solution.

What's a notched jig? It's simply a piece of wood with parallel sides and a shape cut out along one of its edges. The cutout, or notch, may be the shape of the part that you need, as would be the case if you required small wedges, or it may be the shape of the waste piece that will be removed, as would be the case if you were making a taper cut.

The jig, moved along the rip fence, acts as both a carrier for the work and a gauge for the cut. Thus, you can position workpieces precisely even when unusual shapes are required.

When do jigs of this type make sense?

- When a component is too small for safe handling.
- When the shape of a part makes it impractical to produce by conventional means.
- When you need many small, identical pieces.
- When a slight error is magnified because the same cut must be re-

Shown here is the taper jig.

peated on multiple parts. An example would be a jig to cut frames with mitered corners. In such cases, you don't have to be off more than a degree or so to be frustrated at assembly time. The seemingly insignificant error is multiplied by eight!

Of course, if it's to do its job right, the jig must be made accurately. If you

need just a piece or two, making a special device may not be worth the trouble. In such cases it might be more practical to lay out the shape of the part, rough cut it, then sand it to perfect shape. But for production output and when faced with a cut that might put fingers in jeopardy, opt for a notched jig — like one of those shown in the illustrations.

Tips

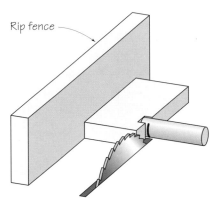

- Jigs don't have to be fancy, but notches must be accurate.
- Make the jigs wide enough to provide ample room for your hand.
- Be sure the rip fence and saw blade are parallel.

Four Great Dowel Jigs

DOWEL-NOTCHING JIG

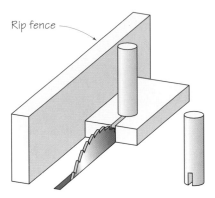

Rip fence

In this case, the "notch" is simply a hole in a carrier board that holds the cylinder or dowel in the correct position for the cut.

DOWEL-CUTTING JIG

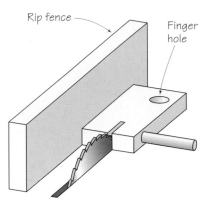

Rip fence

Finger hole

Cut dowels to length accurately and with a minimum of feathering. The finger hole is for pulling back the jig after the dowel is cut.

DOWEL DISC JIG

Rip fence

Cut the discs from dowels, a closet pole or lathe-turned cylinders. The notch is just wide enough to hold work firmly. The notch's depth equals the thickness of the required discs.

DOWEL DISC-SECTIONING JIG

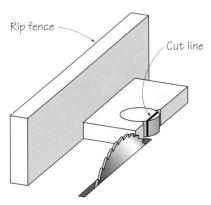

Rip fence

Cut line

Cut sections from discs. A V-notch would also work, but it would be more difficult to control the piece.

OCTAGON JIG

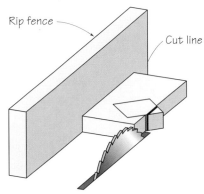

Rip fence

Cut line

Odd-shaped pieces, such as octagons, can be cut from squares held in a notched jig so corners can be removed. Form the notch on a scroll saw or band saw.

Shown here is the wedge jig.

After drawing the shape of the taper for either the taper jig or the wedge jig, make the short cut first.

Then make the long cut.

Two Great Angle Jigs

TAPER JIG

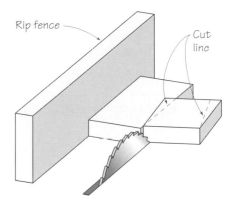

Rip fence

Cut line

For tapers, the notch in the jig is the shape of the waste piece. For the same taper on the opposite side, flip the stock and make a second cut.

WEDGE JIG

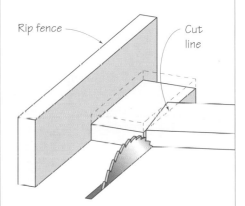

Rip fence

Cut line

For wedges, the notch shape is the shape of the wedge. Make the cut with the point entering the saw blade first. For extra safety, add a ¼"-thick rectangle to the top of the jig covering the notch. This lessens the chance of kickback.

from Popular Woodworking magazine

Tricks of the Trade shares readers' tips for making woodworking tasks easier and safer. All of the tips on this page were submitted by Dick Dorn of Oelwein, Iowa.

tricks *of the* TRADE

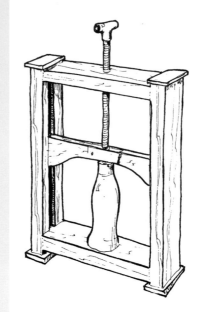

PLYWOOD SHOP PRESS

Sometimes clamps just can't do a proper job, so I built a press from laminated scrap plywood. A press is ideal for clamping such projects as lamps or pedestal tables. The rectangular frame has a groove in the vertical sides that guides the horizontal stabilizer and prevents the screw from twisting the work. The 1" screw turns through a nut that is welded to a steel plate, which is in turn secured to the frame. Adding casters to the bottom eases moving the press around the shop.

REMOVING SPLINTERS WITH GLUE

I recently had a small splinter go straight into my finger. If I have to get splinters, I prefer the type I can remove with tweezers, but I couldn't see this one and it was painful when I touched it. So I ignored the little pest and continued with a large, time-consuming glue-up. When I had finished, I had several layers of dried glue on my fingers.

As I washed up and peeled the glue off my fingers, I noticed the little splinter was gone. Apparently the glue had adhered to the wood and the sliver was pulled out when I pulled off the dried glue.

BISCUIT SLOTS FOR TABLETOPS

I use my biscuit joiner to cut neat slots for metal tabletop fasteners. The #0 setting is perfect. The normal procedure is to cut a full-length groove, but that weakens the apron.

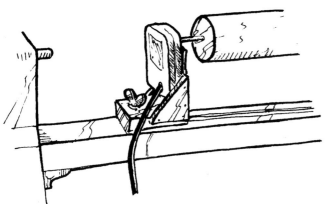

5 RPM BARBECUE LATHE

An old rotisserie motor attached to the bed of a lathe turns the work slowly enough so you can paint turned pieces by hand or with a spray gun.

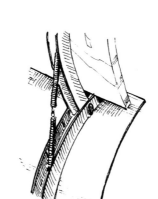

QUIETING RATTLES WITH SPRINGS

My lathe shield rattles — especially when I have it in the raised position while sanding. I attached a pair of springs to the existing assembly bolts. Springs also work well to quiet the rattle in the door.

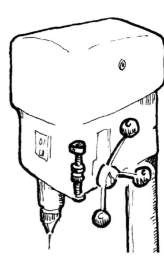

PREVENT LOST STOP-ROD NUTS

I use a ⅝" collar with a set screw at the very top of the stop-rod on my drill press. The collar prevents the nuts for the depth-set gauge from working themselves up the threads, then falling to the floor and getting lost.

22½° ON A RADIAL-ARM SAW

I was making an 8-sided form recently and I noticed that the graduations on my radial-arm saw seemed to have grown together. To check my 22½° setting, I placed my square against the fence and put a 45° triangle in the corner. I then placed a small block of scrap against the triangle and adjusted the overhead arm so the blade was flat against the wood. When everything was set, I cut two small pieces and test fit them against the square and the triangle.

Jim Johnson, Brunswick, Ohio

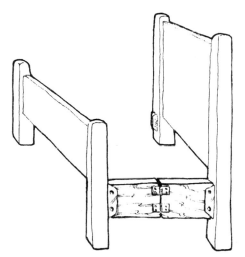

BED FINISHING HELPER

This short, hinged bed rail lets you varnish the headboard and footboards without taking up a lot of room space.

A half set of rail ends is surface-mounted to a 12" hinged rail. The bed can then be opened so you can access all the surfaces while you finish.

*Alice and Robert Tupper,
Canton, South Dakota*

RESIN BATH

At the end of each day, I like to clean any router or drill bits I've used during the day. Mineral spirits have a tendency to split and crack my skin, so I built this bit bath. Use a 39-ounce (no. 10) coffee can and ¼" hardware cloth cut to fit the diameter of the can. Install three 1½" × ¼" bolts around the perimeter of the screen for feet. Place a washer on the top and bottom of the screen and secure with a nut. Use a 6" × ¼" bolt for the handle. Soak the bits overnight; then clean them with a small brass brush.

Tom Lavallee, Salmon, Idaho

SURGICAL CLAMP

After visiting my doctor for a blood test, I bought a flat rubber tourniquet like the one he used. I use it to clamp odd-shaped pieces. The rubber is tough, clamps well and doesn't slip when knotted.

*Alice and Robert Tupper,
Canton, South Dakota*

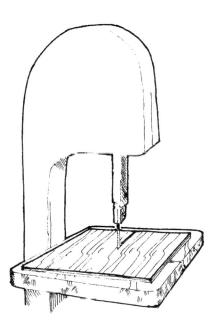

BAND SAW AID

When cutting small pieces on my band saw, they would sometimes fall through the gap in the table insert. To prevent this, I cut a piece of thin plywood to the approximate size of the tabletop and fed it halfway into the blade. An out-of-the-way clamp secures it to the table. The small slit in the top also makes it safer for your fingers.

*John Schluttenhoffer, Earl Park,
Indiana*

Circles Without a Band Saw

Cut circles and even bowls with these three great jigs for your table saw.

You can cut perfect circles — even bowls — on your table saw using these three jigs and what I call the "pivot-guidance technique." This technique is the same for all three jigs. With each, the workpiece rests on a pivot point, and you turn the work over the blade, making light passes until you reach the desired shape.

PERFECT CIRCLES

This jig is great for transforming a square piece of wood into a round one. You start by removing the bulk of the waste stock by making tangent cuts, a chore with a miter gauge and not something to do freehand. But the operation proceeds quickly and safely with a simple jig — just a platform kerfed for the saw blade and guided by a strip that rides in the table slot.

Prepare a piece of plywood for the platform and use a strip of hardwood for the guide (see the drawing titled "Platform for Tangent Cuts"). Set the rip fence 6" from the blade and run a kerf in the platform about 15" long. Leave the platform in place while you slip the guide strip into position. Hold the guide in place by tack-nailing through the platform. Then invert the assembly and attach the guide permanently with glue and short screws or ¾" nails.

The jig is used for the tangent cuts and for the final pivot pass that results in a true circular component. During the entire operation, mount the work on the platform with a nail driven through the center of the work and into the platform. If you don't want a hole through the work, drive the pivot nail up through the platform so it only partially penetrates the bottom of the work.

To make tangent cuts, hold the work securely and move both the jig and the work past the blade. Make repeat passes, rotating the work after each one. The more of this you do, the less work on the final pivot pass.

After the bulk of the waste is removed, clamp the jig to the table so the center line of the work is in line with the front edge of the blade. Then rotate the work slowly counterclockwise. Smoothest cuts result when you work slowly and have done enough tangent cutting to leave a minimum for the final rotation pass.

Cutting a circle directly, skipping the tangent cuts, is also possible. On thin material you can get through in a single pass, but thick material will require repeat passes, raising the blade 1/16" or so after each.

The jig can also be used to shape multisided figures. Draw a line on the platform at right angles to the saw blade, and mark the work so it can be positioned accurately for each of the passes required. An octagon, for example, requires two perpendicular diameters.

I like to get as much as I can out of whatever tool I buy or make, so I view the circular-sawing jig as a sliding table. Here's an example of an extra function I get from the jig: I use it to form short tapers. The work is positioned by a guide that is tack-nailed to the platform. In this case, taper all four sides simply by flipping the stock after each pass.

ROTARY COVING

If you have ever done coving on a table saw you know it's done by making a series of oblique passes across the blade with blade projection increased a bit after each pass. Because of the oblique feed, the profile that results is more a section of an ellipse than a true arc.

To get a true arc (relative to the size of the saw blade), the work has to be moved on a line 90° to the face of the blade. This is feasible, but more important is that it leads to rotary coving, a technique in which the work is situated directly over the saw blade and pivot-guided through repeat passes to produce a bowl shape.

The repeated passes plus the slow rotation of the work may seem a tedious procedure, but it's not. With a 10" blade and a 3" maximum projection, it takes me 4 to 5 minutes to produce a bowl shape about 10" across and 3" deep — not out of line when considering the same type of work done on a lathe. And the rotary technique produces a perfect shape.

There are factors that affect the

Sawing Circles

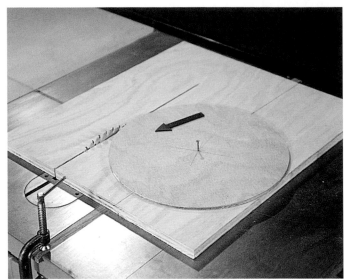

To create a circular component, first make tangent cuts to remove the bulk of the waste stock. Both the work and the jig are moved past the saw blade in repeat passes with the work rotated after each pass. Although not shown in the photographs, use the guard.

After the waste is removed, clamp the jig so the center line of the work is in line with the front edge of the saw blade. Then hold the work firmly and rotate it slowly against the blade's direction of rotation. Set the blade height so it's adequate for the thickness of the stock.

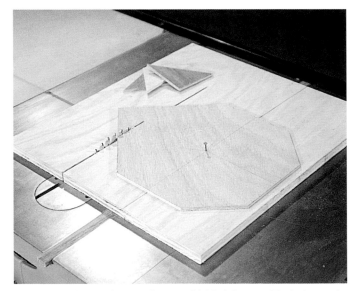

The jig can be used to produce multisided figures. Mark the work for the number of sides needed so it can be aligned with a line on the platform that is at a right angle to the blade. An octagon, for example, requires two perpendicular diameters.

Get more from your jig. Here, I'm forming short tapers on legs I needed for a low stool. The guide, which positions the work for the cuts, is tack-nailed to the platform.

time element. Pine cuts faster than maple, and a saw blade with set teeth cuts faster than, say, a crosscut blade. The blade I use is the one that's usually on my machine: a carbide-tipped combination blade. By making reasonable cuts — not more than $1/16$" or so for each pass — and making the final pass with the blade barely touching the work, I get impressively smooth results.

Because the work covers the blade, you can't see what's happening so it's critical to know the blade projection that results with a turn of the elevating crank. On my machine, a quarter turn of the crank increases blade projection about $1/8$", so I know how many full turns of the crank I need to get to a particular depth.

However, should you get lost, it's

simple to remove the work from the jig being used and make a visual check.

Also be sure your starting block is of sufficient size to suit the blade used and the size of the depression you plan.

THE JIG YOU NEED

I use this idea for inside cuts (bowl shapes) and perimeter cuts. Two different jigs perform the two different cuts.

The overhead jig, shown in the drawing titled "Coving Jig," is for bowl shapes. It's sized so I can rotate a 3½"-thick by 12"-square block under the pivot screw.

Start the project by sizing the platform and making two guide bars to suit the slots in the saw table. Set the rip fence so the platform will be centered over the blade, and slip the guide bars into place. Secure the guides by driving ⅜" brads through the platform. If you want, remove the guides and reinstall them after applying glue. Now raise the blade with the assembly in place and form a centered kerf about 11" long.

Make the verticals by first tack-nailing together the two pieces. Next cut the slants on the sides and form the U-shape required for the bar on both pieces. You can form the U-shape with a dado if you use a miter gauge with an extension that will provide adequate support for the work. Size the U to provide a tight fit for the bar.

Now separate the pieces and form the rabbet cut along the base of each of them. Attach the parts to the platform with glue and ¾" brads that are driven up through the platform. Be sure the vertical pieces are centered on the platform.

Cut the bar to size and drill a ¼" hole in its center. Install the insert and place the bar with glue, being sure the insert is exactly over the kerf in the platform. Make the pivot as suggested in the drawing or use a ready-made 6" eyebolt.

IN USE

Clamp the jig so the pivot is centered over the saw blade. Workpieces are prepared with a slight, exactly centered countersink for the pivot point to rest in. Thread the pivot down until it sits in the countersink, tight enough to hold the work firmly but allow it to be rotated. Then tighten up the locknut to secure the setting. Work of any size — round or square — can be established with the jig.

Variations are possible so long as you remember there is a critical relationship between the size of the work and the diameter of the blade.

PLATFORM FOR TANGENT CUTS

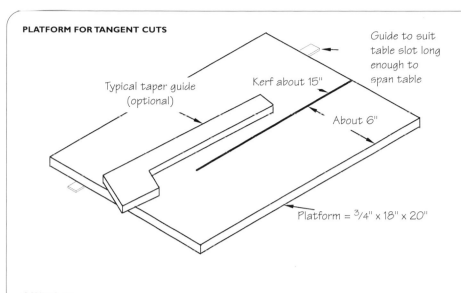

Typical taper guide (optional)

Kerf about 15"

Guide to suit table slot long enough to span table

About 6"

Platform = ³/4" x 18" x 20"

COVING JIG

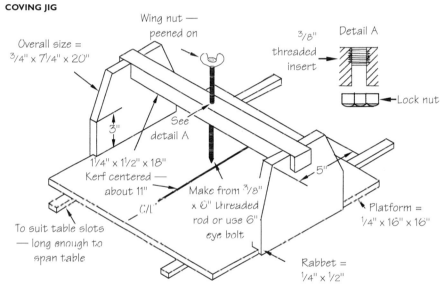

Wing nut — peened on

Overall size = ³/4" x 7¼" x 20"

3"

See detail A

1¼" x 1½" x 18" Kerf centered — about 11"

C/L

To suit table slots — long enough to span table

Make from ³/8" x 6" threaded rod or use 6" eye bolt

³/8" threaded insert

Detail A

Lock nut

5"

Platform = ¼" x 16" x 16"

Rabbet = ¼" x ½"

VARIATIONS — INSIDE CUTS

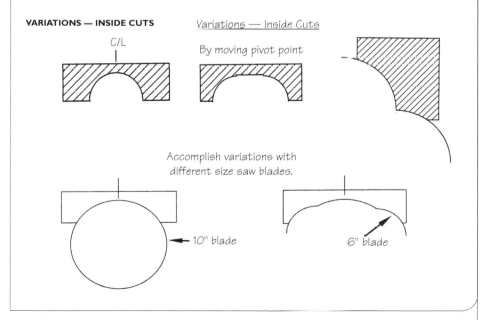

C/L

Variations — Inside Cuts

By moving pivot point

Accomplish variations with different size saw blades.

10" blade

6" blade

Rotary Coving

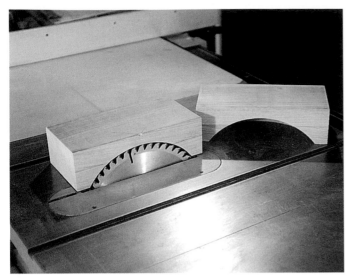

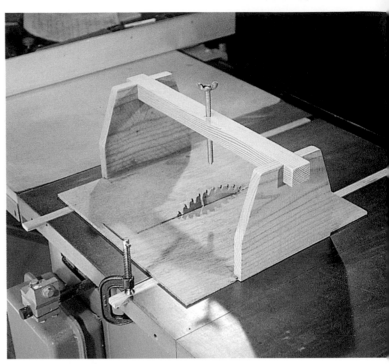

Output from a 10" blade includes a bowl shape almost 10" across and 3" deep. The starting block can be square, round or even rectangular, just as long as the size can be handled by the jig.

The overhead jig is centered over the saw blade and clamped in place. The jig, as dimensioned, can be used with workpieces up to 12" square and about 4" thick.

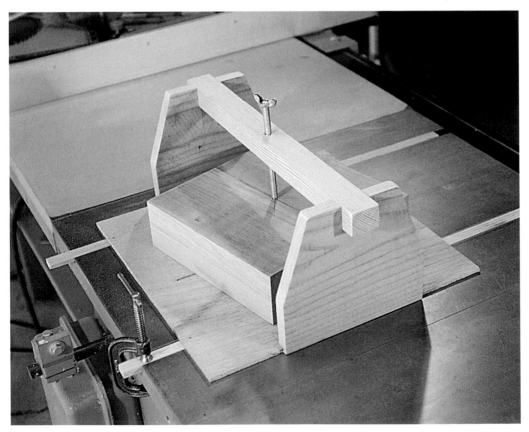

Secure workpieces with the pivot point (the piece shown is a bit too large for the jig). Adjust the pivot so the work is held firmly but will rotate. Secure the pivot setting with a locknut.

Perimeter Cuts

JIG FOR PERIMETER CUTS

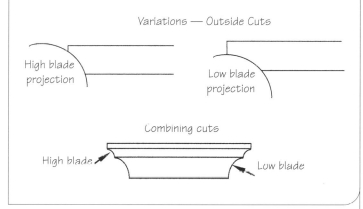

Perimeter shaping is done with the flat jig. The workpiece is secured on a pivot and supported by the V-block. The procedure is standard: Repeat passes with the blade raised a bit after each one.

Here the jig is clamped in place, and the position of the pivot point and V-block are established. Because the blade is exposed, be sure to use the saw's guard.

PERIMETER CUTS

Outside cuts, like the one shown in the photos above, are feasible on round projects, but the procedure calls for the jig shown in the drawing titled "Jig for Perimeter Cuts." Make the jig by following the steps suggested for the overhead jig. Start with the platform and center it over the saw blade by using the rip fence, then add the guide bars. The V-block is an optional but wise addition because it can supply security when doing the work. Also, the V-block can add to the jig's function. For example, use it to make miter cuts on frame components that have been precut to length.

Like inside cuts, perimeter shapes are produced by making repeat passes with the saw blade raised a bit after each one. The shape you get is affected by the size of the saw blade, where the jig is clamped and the placement of the pivot point.

Approach this area of pivot work carefully because the saw blade is exposed, so be sure to use the saw guard! Even with the guard in place, don't use the technique on projects smaller than 6" in diameter.

Believe it or not, making an integral round tenon is a practical application on a jointer, but you must use hold-downs and the proper fixtures. Be aware that the guard isn't used for this technique — so be careful.

Jointers: The Forgotten Power Tool

If you think jointers are just good for giving you a true edge on a board, you don't know the half of it.

A shop teacher of long ago told me that the second tool to buy (after a table saw) was a jointer. I took his advice and have never regretted it, and I often wonder why some shops lack the tool.

My teacher showed us the "working edge" philosophy: Establish two smooth, flat surfaces (an edge and a face) that are square to each other before going further with a board. Making a straight, uniform and even surface is called jointing and is done with a jointer. These surfaces are the ones from which all other dimensions are made, and, if the board must be sawed to width, there is a true edge to ride the rip fence. Similarly, if the board must be planed to clean up a rough face or thicknessed to a given dimension, there is a "true" surface to run on the planer's table.

But the reason I'm so happy to own this tool is that there's so much more to a jointer than this basic procedure. I don't know if my shop teacher was aware of it or not, but using a jointer only for edge or face jointing is like using a table saw just for ripping and crosscutting. After becoming familiar with the machine, you'll find it practical for chores ranging from simple edge-planing to forming tenons on round stock (drawing 1).

THE TOOL

A jointer consists of a horizontal cutterhead (usually with two or three knives) mounted beneath and between the "infeed" and "outfeed" tables. The length of the knives determines the tool's size and the maximum width of stock that can be surfaced, 6" being a reasonable choice for home shops. The depth of cut that the machine can make on a single pass, which can range from $\frac{1}{16}$" to $\frac{1}{2}$", is established by the vertical adjustment of the infeed table.

On some units, both tables are adjustable. And while this affects the procedures you use to align the knives and the tables, it has only a minimal effect on the work you can do. Standard equipment on all jointers is a fence that can be tilted and moved across the tables. Except for chores like chamfering or beveling, the angle between the fence and tables must be 90°.

The horizontal plane of the outfeed table must be tangent to the cutting circle of the knives. Check this by placing a straightedge on the table so it extends over the cutterhead. Rotate the head by hand. Each knife should just barely touch the straightedge. Because jointer designs differ, follow the instructions in your owner's manual for making this critical adjustment. When the relationship is correct, work will pass smoothly over the cutterhead and firmly onto the rear table (drawing 2).

RABBETS AND TENONS

The jointer is an excellent tool for rabbeting and tenoning. It produces cuts with flat, smooth cheeks and square shoulders. I choose the jointer over a dadoing tool for this kind of work. The width of a rabbet is established by the position of the fence; its depth, by adjustment of the infeed table. Place the work firmly on the rabbeting ledge and snugly against the fence, then advance it past the cutterhead. A clamped hold-down aids in producing accurate results (photo 1). To form a tongue, flip the stock and make a second cut (photo 2).

Tenons are just back-to-back rabbet cuts. But because they are made crossgrain, you can expect some tear-out at the end of the cut (photo 3). Therefore, start with wood that is a bit wider than you need so you can rip off any imperfections. When you need several similar tenons, do the initial shaping on wide stock and then rip the parts you need to width. Use a backup to move the work when forming tenons on narrow stock — and use a clamped hold-down to keep the work in position.

BEVELS AND CHAMFERS

The jointer fence can be tilted in either direction, but I prefer to use a closed angle because it provides a nook that snugs the work and helps maintain its position during the pass.

The addition of a hold-in is also a good idea (photo 4). It's usually necessary to make more than one pass to achieve a full bevel. Chamfer cuts are made the same way, the only difference being that you don't remove the entire edge of the stock.

TAPERING

To do a simple taper, set the infeed table for a particular depth of cut and then position the work so the starting point of the taper rests on the forward edge of the outfeed table. It's a fairly simple procedure so long as the workpiece isn't longer than the infeed table (drawing 3). For longer work, a different procedure is followed. Mark the working divisions that are shorter than the length of the infeed table and divide the depth of the cut into an equal number of divisions. For example, if the board is 24" long and you need to taper it ½", mark the center point of the board and set your depth of cut to ¼". Make one cut from the center mark, then a second cut from the end of the board.

Tapering is one situation where a long fence can be handy. A long board clamped to the regular fence can help, but a special one that can be a permanent accessory is better. The one I made for my 6" jointer is adjustable and incorporates a stop that's needed when doing some other type of jointer work (drawing 4). Some jointers have holes bored through the fence that are perfect for this accessory.

Short tapers are formed by standing at the rear of the machine and pulling the work across the knives as shown in photo 5. Start by lowering the infeed table for the depth of your cut and placing the work over the knives where the cut must start. Use a stop block to establish that position and place a suitable height block under the aft end of the work. The block can be clamped to the table, but this will result in a slight curve running the length of the taper. If the block is attached to the work so that the two pieces move together, the taper will be flat. I do this by using double-sided carpet tape to keep the

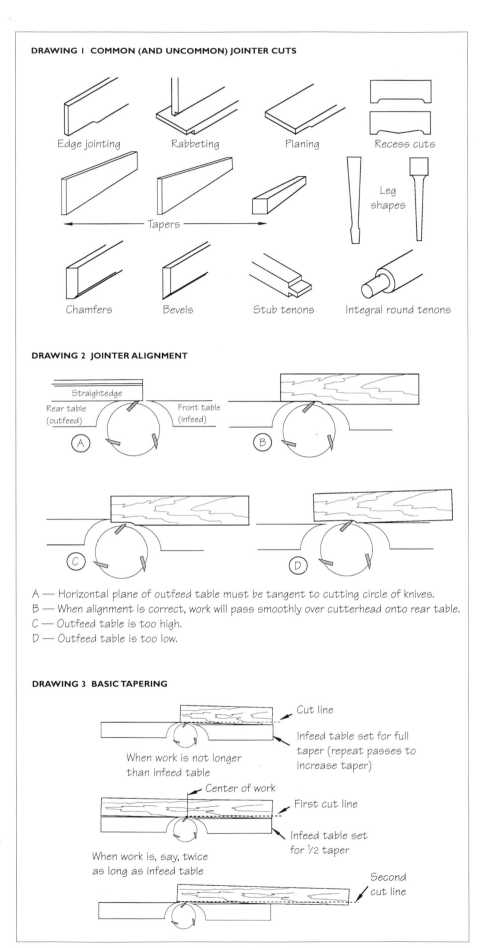

DRAWING 1 COMMON (AND UNCOMMON) JOINTER CUTS

Edge jointing   Rabbeting   Planing   Recess cuts

Leg shapes

Tapers

Chamfers   Bevels   Stub tenons   Integral round tenons

DRAWING 2 JOINTER ALIGNMENT

Straightedge
Rear table (outfeed)   Front table (infeed)

A   B

C   D

A — Horizontal plane of outfeed table must be tangent to cutting circle of knives.
B — When alignment is correct, work will pass smoothly over cutterhead onto rear table.
C — Outfeed table is too high.
D — Outfeed table is too low.

DRAWING 3 BASIC TAPERING

Cut line

Infeed table set for full taper (repeat passes to increase taper)

When work is not longer than infeed table

Center of work

First cut line

Infeed table set for ½ taper

When work is, say, twice as long as infeed table

Second cut line

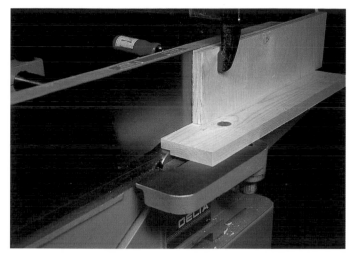

1 I use the jointer for rabbeting more than any other machine. Cuts are smooth and precise and the machine is easy to set up for the chore. A clamped block helps keep the work flat on the table. Because you have to remove the guard, be especially careful with where you put your hands.

2 A tongue is formed by inverting the stock and making a second pass. Adjust the clamped hold-down block to suit.

3 Tenons are back-to-back rabbet cuts. Because they're run against the grain, some tear-out can occur at the ends of the cut.

height block in place.

Start the cut by placing the work free of the knives and braced against the stop block. Then pull the work toward you after lowering it to contact the knives.

A companion taper, needed to complete the leg shape shown in drawing 1, is formed in the same way. In this case, two stop blocks are used — one to start the cut, the other to control its length (photo 6). The slight roughness at the end of cuts of this type can be easily sanded away.

A type of leg shape that requires a similar reduction on four sides of the parent stock is another jointer function (photo 7). It's like making surfacing cuts of limited length. The work is placed on the infeed table and moved forward until it contacts the stop block.

RECESSING

A recessing cut is good for cabinet bases and bottoms of table and stand legs. If both tables of your jointer are

adjustable, then lower them for the depth of the cut you want to take and make the cut in one pass. If the rear table is fixed, then make a second pass after the stock has been reversed (photo 8). This leaves a raised center that can remain as an added detail or it can be ripped off your stock. In either case, use two stop blocks — one to brace against the start of the cut, the other to control the cut's length.

4 The jointer makes perfectly smooth bevels and chamfers. I prefer to work with the fence at an acute angle (less than 90°).

5 Form short tapers by bracing your leg against a stop block and pulling it across the knives. Use a hold-down to keep the work in place as you pull it for the cut. Always keep the guard in place, even though it isn't shown in these photos.

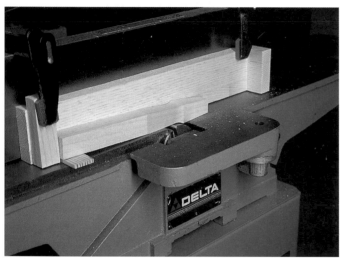

6 A companion taper to complete the leg shape is formed the same way. In this case use two stop blocks. Brace the work firmly against the front stop block before you lower it for the cut. A small nail tapped in the aft end of the stock will make the leg easier to pull across the knives.

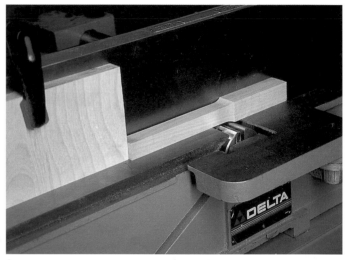

7 A leg shape that needs to be reduced in size for a limited length is a straightforward chore for the jointer. The work is placed on the infeed table and moved forward until it contacts the stop block. Then the cut is repeated on the remaining three sides.

8 This photo shows a recessing cut with only the infeed table lowered. The second cut is made after reversing the stock's position.

9 The jig in the drawing above makes round tenons easier than you might think.

10 Frequent honing of the knives will keep them sharp. Wrapping most of the stone will prevent it from scratching the table.

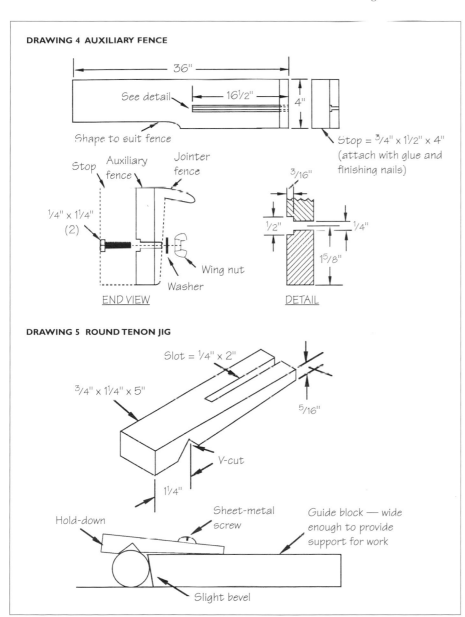

DRAWING 4 AUXILIARY FENCE

36"

See detail

16½"

4"

Shape to suit fence

Stop = ¾" x 1½" x 4"
(attach with glue and finishing nails)

Stop   Auxiliary   Jointer
        fence   fence

¼" x 1¼"
(2)

Wing nut

Washer

END VIEW

3/16"

½"   ¼"

1⁵/8"

DETAIL

DRAWING 5 ROUND TENON JIG

Slot = ¼" x 2"

¾" x 1¼" x 5"

5/16"

V-cut

1¼"

Hold-down

Sheet-metal
screw

Guide block — wide
enough to provide
support for work

Slight bevel

ROUND TENONS

The jointer can form integral tenons on round stock, but the job must be done carefully and with the jig in drawing 5. Lock the fence in place to gauge the length of the tenon, and set the jig's hold-down so it secures the work while still allowing you to turn it (photo 9). With the machine on, move the work forward slowly until it meets the fence and then turn it in a clockwise direction. The density of the material will affect how deep you can cut. In any case you will get better results by getting there in stages.

Don't use this technique on small-diameter dowels or on short pieces. If you need short components, start with stock that is long enough for safe handling and then saw off the part you need.

HONING KNIVES

Frequent and careful honing of your knives will keep them keen for a long time. To hone them, first unplug the machine, cover part of a fine Carborundum stone with paper and place it on the infeed table as shown in photo 10. Raise the table and rotate the cutterhead by hand until the stone rests flat on the bevel of the knife. Stroke the knife lengthwise four or five times. Hone each of the knives with the same number of strokes.

Edge-jointing is a primary jointer function. Position yourself and
your hands so you can make the pass smoothly from start to finish.
Several light cuts are usually better than a single heavy one.

Jointing With Accuracy

A smart start leads to quality results.

If you study the owner's manual of your jointer, as you should, you'll find a statement that says something like, "This machine has been checked at the factory for accurate results, but ..."

That "but" is something to heed because a lot can happen between the statement and setting up the tool in your shop. What causes your tool to become misaligned during shipment isn't important; being sure the machine will work with you, is.

CHECKING

The horizontal plane of the outfeed table must be tangential to the cutting circle of the knives (diagram 1). Check for accuracy by placing a straightedge on the table so it extends over the cutterhead. Rotate the cutterhead by hand (tool unplugged), and determine if each knife just barely touches the straightedge. Because the knives must also be parallel to the tables, make the check at each end of the knives. Jointer designs differ, so refer to the owner's manual for instructions concerning adjustments that might be necessary. I'll talk more about this phase of jointer maintenance when I address knife sharpening. Anyway, you'll know as soon as you start working whether the relationship is correct. Work should pass smoothly over the cutterhead and firmly onto the rear table. This will not happen if the knives are too high or too low (diagram 1).

THE FENCE

The angle between the fence and the tables must be 90° when the fence is locked at its 0 setting. Check the angle with a square or a draftsman's template, and, if necessary, make a correction by adjusting the setting's auto-stop. Repeat the procedure with the fence tilted to 45°. There might also be stops at 22½° and 30°. Their accuracy can be determined later when you're at work and those angles are called for.

In all cases, final judgment of accuracy is determined by checking actual cuts with a protractor or a square.

DEPTH OF CUT

Carefully mark a piece of stock ⅛" from its edge and make a partial test-cut. When you are sure the cut is correct, adjust the pointer on the depth-of-cut scale to exactly ⅛". If the pointer has a round end, and they usually do, file it to a point (diagram 2). Reestablish this setting anytime the knives are replaced.

AT WORK

Edge-jointing is the most common operation done on the jointer. Use both hands to hold the work firmly down on the infeed table and snug against the fence. As the cut progresses, move your left hand to keep the work down on the outfeed table while your right hand merely moves the work forward.

Some operators object to passing either hand over the cutterhead, but this can result in some awkward positions, especially on long pieces of work. Actually, there is little danger involved in ignoring the advice so long as you stay alert, are sure the guard is working properly and don't attempt to joint pieces that are too narrow for safe hand positions.

Use a depth-of-cut setting that gets the job done; the less, the better, even if you must make repeat passes to achieve the edge you want. Several light passes are usually better than a single heavy one.

JOINTING END GRAIN

If you joint the end of a board in one pass, it's inevitable that a portion of the wood will split off at the end of the pass. Avoid the problem by using a two-pass technique. That is, advance the work over the cutterhead only an inch or so, and then reverse the stock and make a second, complete pass (diagram 3). When jointing four edges, follow the sequence of passes that are suggested in the drawing. The idea is that your with-the-grain cuts will remove the imperfections caused by your cross-grained cuts.

If you are working with plywood — and you can if you keep your depth of cut to a minimum — judge the grain direction of the surface veneer as if you were working with solid stock.

DIAGRAM I ALIGNMENT

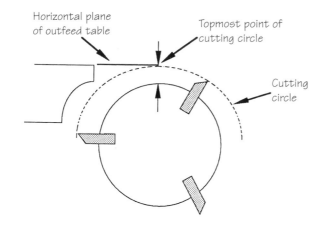

Horizontal plane of outfeed table

Topmost point of cutting circle

Cutting circle

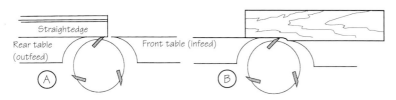

Straightedge

Rear table (outfeed)

Front table (infeed)

(A) (B)

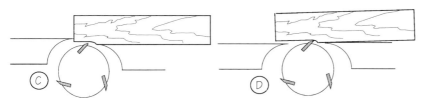

(C) (D)

A — Horizontal plane of outfeed table must be tangent to cutting circle of knives.
B — When alignment is correct, work will pass smoothly over cutterhead onto rear table.
C — Outfeed table is too high.
D — Outfeed table is too low.

DIAGRAM 2 SETTING A DEPTH GAUGE

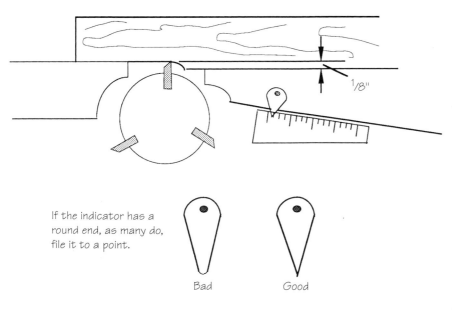

1/8"

If the indicator has a round end, as many do, file it to a point.

Bad   Good

It's good practice to occasionally move the position of the fence so as not to overuse one area of the knives. Be aware that this exposes the knives behind the fence, which is why I recommend getting a second guard. Most jointers will permit mounting a guard behind the fence so the knives will be covered fore and aft.

SURFACING

Surfacing is usually done to smooth a rough surface or, if you don't have a planer, to reduce the stock's thickness. The chore requires more consideration than simple edge-jointing or face-jointing. For one thing, a lot more material is removed so keep depth of cut to a minimum. It's critical to maintain uniform contact with the tables throughout the pass to avoid tapered cuts, gouges and generally imperfect results. Signs that you are not "on track" are work chatter or an obvious decrease in cutterhead rpm. When these symptoms occur, you are probably cutting too deep or too fast.

Successful surfacing requires a tool that combines a pusher with a hold-down. Such an accessory, which you can make, does more than help do a good job; it provides an extra degree of safety because it automatically keeps your hands away from the cutterhead.

It's good practice to have a couple of pusher hold-downs available; the major difference between them is in length and grip design (diagram 4). The longer type allows the use of both hands to keep the work in good contact with the jointer tables. Each of them has a ¼"-thick "cleat" at the pusher end so the tool can't be used on thin material — a good precaution since it isn't wise to surface very thin stock.

In some cases, for example, long work, the pusher hold-downs are not ideal. I have two solutions you might consider. With one, I place the work on the infeed table and clamp a strip of wood to the fence so it bears down on the workpiece just enough to keep it in contact with the tables.

My second idea is a roller-type

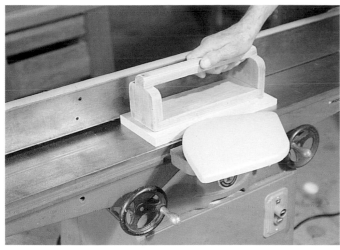

Successful surface planing requires that the work be kept flat on the tables throughout the pass. Combination pusher hold-downs help accomplish this while they keep your hands well away from the cutting area. Here, more so than in edge-jointing, light cuts are good practice.

This photo shows another way to keep work flat on the tables when doing surfacing. Position the strip of wood so it bears down just enough to maintain the work in proper position. The strip does not interfere with using a pusher.

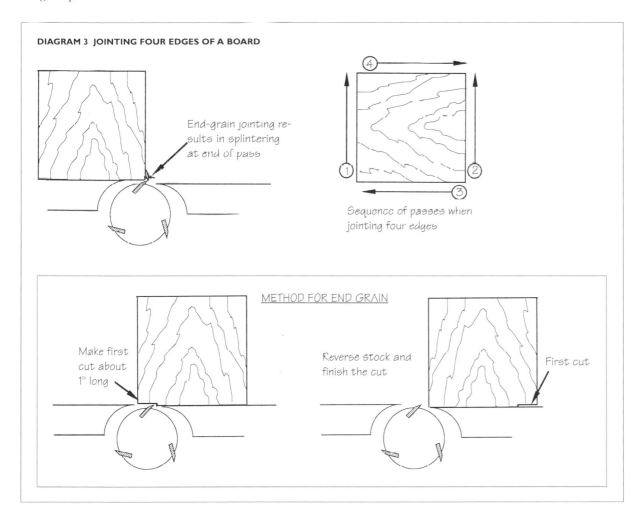

DIAGRAM 3 JOINTING FOUR EDGES OF A BOARD

End-grain jointing results in splintering at end of pass

Sequence of passes when jointing four edges

METHOD FOR END GRAIN

Make first cut about 1" long

Reverse stock and finish the cut

First cut

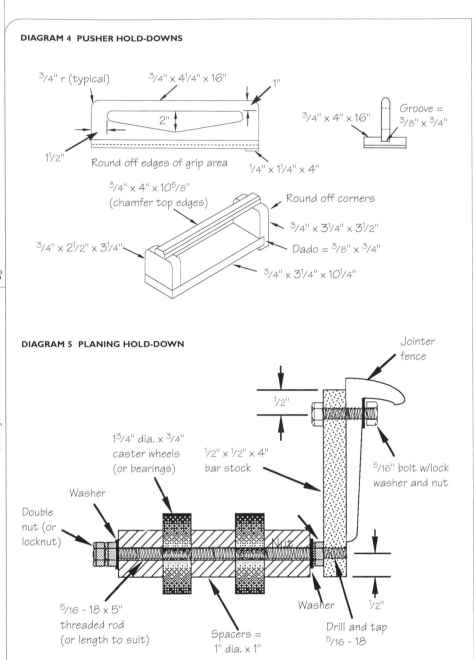

DIAGRAM 4 PUSHER HOLD-DOWNS

3/4" r (typical)
3/4" x 4 1/4" x 16"
1"
2"
1 1/2"
Round off edges of grip area
3/4" x 4" x 16"
Groove = 3/8" x 3/4"
1/4" x 1 1/4" x 4"

3/4" x 4" x 10 5/8"
(chamfer top edges)
Round off corners
3/4" x 3 1/4" x 3 1/2"
Dado = 3/8" x 3/4"
3/4" x 2 1/2" x 3 1/4"
3/4" x 3 1/4" x 10 1/4"

DIAGRAM 5 PLANING HOLD-DOWN

Jointer fence
1/2"
1 3/4" dia. x 3/4" caster wheels (or bearings)
1/2" x 1/2" x 4" bar stock
5/16" bolt w/lock washer and nut
Washer
Double nut (or locknut)
5/16 - 18 x 5" threaded rod (or length to suit)
Spacers = 1" dia. x 1"
Washer
Drill and tap 5/16 - 18
1/2"

hold-down that's secured with a bolt that passes through a custom-drilled hole in the fence over the area of the outfeed table. The unit, made as shown in diagram 5, can be pivoted toward the front or rear of the table. In use, I advance the work just far enough so the hold-down can be locked to bear down on the workpiece enough to keep it flat on the outfeed table.

DISTORTED STOCK

The jointer is most commonly used to make right a piece of stock that isn't flat or straight (diagram 6), but the machine is not always a cure-all. Sometimes you must resort to combining jointer work with cuts on a band saw or table saw. A "dished" or "cupped" board, one that is not wider than the cutterhead knives, can be flattened by following the steps in diagram 7. Make the first pass, or passes, with the concave side down on the table. When flat, the next step is to square an edge by jointing it with the flat face against the fence. The convex surface should be flattened using a planer to ensure you

make it parallel to the jointed face. A board with an edge that's dished along its length can be made usable by first flattening the concave edge with jointer cuts. This provides a straight edge so the piece can be ripped to width by running the straight edge against the saw's fence. The sawn edge can then be smoothed on the jointer.

A board "in wind" (twisted along its length) is usually the hardest problem to correct. If the twist is slight, the board might be dressed by flattening one surface on the jointer and then planing the opposite surface. If the twist is extreme, it's better to use the board for shorter pieces that can be flattened.

In any case, when salvaging distorted stock, you must accept a reduction in the thickness or width of the piece.

HONING KNIVES

Frequent, careful honing of the knives will help them keep for a long time. First unplug the machine, then cover part of a fine Carborundum stone with paper and place it on the infeed table so it projects over the cutterhead. Raise the table and rotate the cutterhead by hand until the stone rests flat on the bevel of the knife. Stroke the knife lengthwise four or five times. Repeat the chore on each of the knives.

GRINDING KNIVES

When knives have been nicked or are beyond sharpening by honing, the cutting bevel must be reground. The work can be accomplished fairly easily on a drill press or disc sander (diagrams 8 and 9). In each case you need a holder that has a groove that will hold the knife firmly and at the correct angle. When necessary, a strip of paper or screws can be used to secure the knife. Always be sure each knife is bedded in the groove.

Work with a fine-grit cup-type grinding wheel on the drill press. Position the guide strip so only the edge of the grinding wheel is used. Lock the quill so the grinder makes very light contact with the knife. Note that the drill press table is tilted at a slight

I use my custom-designed roller-type hold-down to keep the work down on the outfeed table when surface planing long stock. Bearings can be used in place of the wheels, which I salvaged from casters.

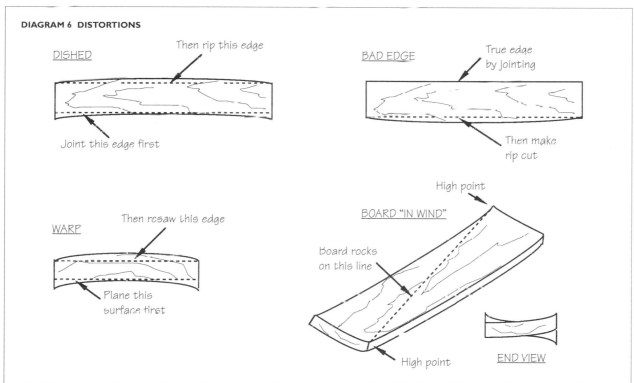

DIAGRAM 6 DISTORTIONS

DISHED
Then rip this edge
Joint this edge first

BAD EDGE
True edge by jointing
Then make rip cut

WARP
Then resaw this edge
Plane this surface first

BOARD "IN WIND"
High point
Board rocks on this line
High point
END VIEW

angle, which provides further insurance that only the edge of the cup will contact the knife.

The blade-holder arrangement is moved from left to right and lifted from the table at the end of the pass. If necessary, repeat the procedure after lowering the quill a fraction.

Make the first pass on each knife before making any change. Always wear safety goggles.

The procedure for doing the job on a disc sander is much the same. The guide strip is clamped so there is a slight angle between the forward edge of the disc and the knife. Make the

setup so there is light contact between the disc and the knife. The pass is from right to left and is repeated, if necessary, after repositioning the guide strip.

After grinding, be sure to remove the burr from the edge by drawing the flat side of the knife over an oil stone.

Tip

When face-jointing a board to flatten it, push from the infeed side and use only slight pressure to hold the board down. Let only the fence of the rotating cutterhead draw the board to the outfeed table. Never artificially "straighten" the board by pressing down, as it will only spring back to its warped shape when released.

DIAGRAM 7 FLATTENING DISTORTED STOCK

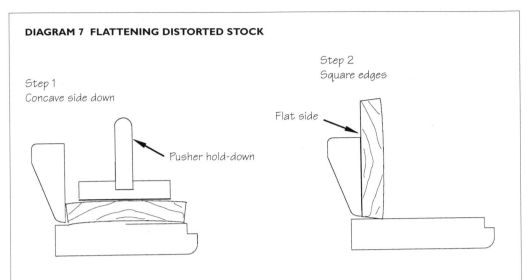

Step 1
Concave side down

Pusher hold-down

Step 2
Square edges

Flat side

DIAGRAM 8 GRINDING KNIVES ON A DRILL PRESS

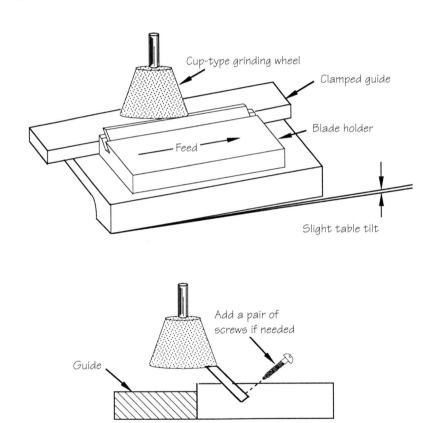

Cup-type grinding wheel

Clamped guide

Blade holder

Feed

Slight table tilt

Add a pair of screws if needed

Guide

RESETTING THE KNIVES

While methods of securing knives in the cutterhead differ, all have one thing in common: The height of the knives must relate correctly to the plane of the table. This can be accomplished by using a straightedge as a guide, but it can be awkward. That's why I made and use the magnetic holder shown in the photo.

The holder is hardwood with flat-bottomed holes that were formed with a Forstner bit. The holes contain flush-set, ⅛"-thick by 1"-diameter button magnets that keep the jig on the table while holding the knives at the correct height.

Shape the jig along the lines shown in diagram 10. Then form the holes ⅛" deep and shape the dado along the center of the forward holes. Use a drop of epoxy to secure the magnets. I obtained the magnets in a hobby shop. If this doesn't work for you, a source of supply is Magnet Sales and Manufacturing, Inc., 11248 Playa Court, Culver City, CA 90230, 800-421-6692, www.magnetsales.com.

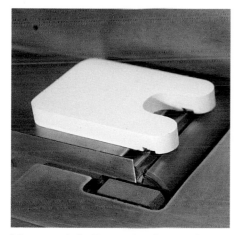

My magnetic knife-resetting jig stays flat on the outfeed table while holding the knife at the correct height. Note the straightedge. It's there so I can set the knives lengthwise to conform with the rabbeting ledge.

Sources for Rare Earth Magnets
- Lee Valley, 800-267-8735
  www.leevalley.com
- Woodcraft, 800-225-1153
  www.woodcraft.com

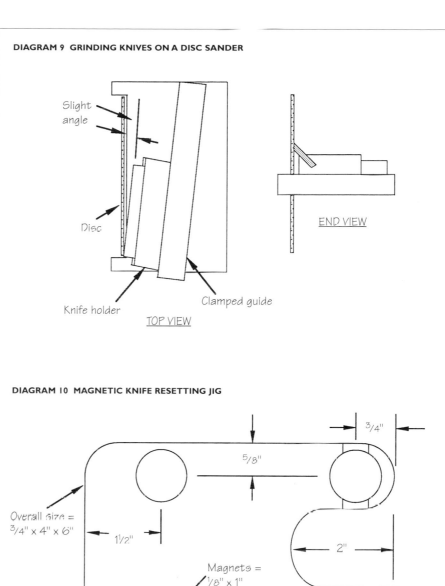

DIAGRAM 9 GRINDING KNIVES ON A DISC SANDER

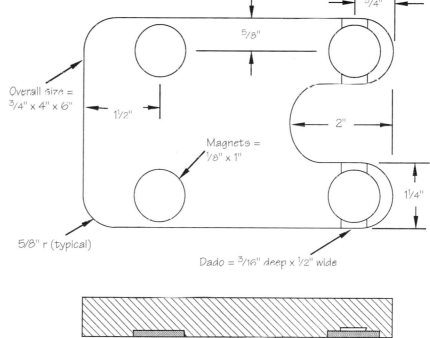

DIAGRAM 10 MAGNETIC KNIFE RESETTING JIG

Put the Mortiser to Work

**Build a workstation, then learn basic and
advanced mortising techniques.**

In this article, I will discuss the advantages of a hollow chisel mortiser versus using accessories for the drill press to form classic mortise-and-tenon joints. The machine is an independent tool that should be bolted to a solid surface for efficiency and safety. It can be fastened to an existing workbench, but there it can interfere with other work, unless you mount it only when it's needed, a method that somewhat thwarts the practicality of the dedicated machine concept.

A better idea is to secure it to its own bench so it will be truly "independent," and ever ready for its joinery functions. The workstation project we designed (diagram 1 with photo inset) is straightforward and compact, needing little more room than the machine itself.

The setup provides considerably more work support than the tool's table, and small drawers are incorporated for handy storage of accessories.

Once organized, the setup provides for efficient production of standard mortise-and-tenon joints and, with a special V-block jig, can be used to form the variations that are often required for furniture projects (photos 1 and 2).

MAKING THE BENCHTOP
Start by cutting the base piece. Be careful when establishing the distance between the dadoes required for the partitions since this space must accom-

1 Conventional stopped or through mortises, side mortises, slots and so on are done in routine fashion, with the special bench providing much more work support than the machine's table.

modate the base of the mortiser (diagram 1A). Next, cut the two partitions and the ends. The width of these components must be exact since, after the tops are added, the total height of the benchtop must equal the height of the tool's base plus ¾".

Install the partitions with glue and 4d nails; the ends with glue and 4d finishing nails. The tops, after being rabbeted, are added to the assembly with glue and 4d finishing nails.

Shape the riser from a piece of hardwood, being sure that its thickness is exactly 1¾". Install it with glue and three No. 8 × 1½" flathead screws run up through the base's underside.

The drawers aren't fancy, but they serve the purpose. Cut all parts to size

(diagram 1B), and then attach the bottom, back and front to the sides with glue and 1" brads. Be sure to bore a centered, 1" finger hole through the drawer front before assembly.

THE STAND
Start the stand (diagram 1C) by cutting the eight pieces for the legs to overall size and then tapering the bottom ends. The slanted cuts can easily be formed with a tapering jig on the table saw, or by using a scroll saw or band saw. Assemble the two-piece legs with glue and 6d finishing nails.

The next step is to make the two top braces and attach each to a pair of legs with glue and 6d finishing nails. Cut the four rails to size and start as-

2 The addition of a V-block jig makes it easy to form mortises in round stock. A typical application is cutting a mortise in a round leg to receive a square or rectangular rail or stretcher.

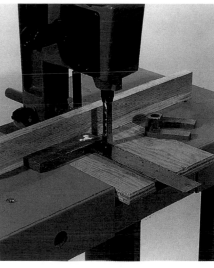

3 The first step when setting up for any mortise is to be sure the angle between the side of the chisel and the fence is 90°. It's a good idea to check this alignment as you go when doing a considerable amount of cutting. Note the centered insert is easily replaceable.

sembly by attaching the end rails, then add the front and back rails. These parts are attached with glue and 4d finishing nails. An alternate method would be to put the four rails together as a subassembly before installation. The final step is to add the shelf, using glue and No. 7 × 1¼" flathead screws.

The stand is secured to the benchtop with glue and No. 10 × 1¼" flathead screws through the underside of the braces. Finishing is optional. The project can be protected with several applications of sealer and left natural or can be coated with spray paint, as I did. Secure the machine with a pair of ⅜" × 3" bolts and nuts. Use flat washers and lock washers under the nuts.

AT WORK

Mortising will be accurate only if you make sure of the alignment between the chisel and fence before you start a job. Checking can be done with a square as shown in photo 3, or by moving the fence forward until the back of the chisel is flush against it. Misalignment is revealed when a mortise has staggered edges.

The bulk of the waste when mortising is removed by the bit, but corners

are squared by the chisel, which is why this type of work requires more downward pressure than does simple drilling. The force required will vary depending on the density of the wood, but let good judgment prevail. Cutting should be consistent, with wood chips spewing freely through the relief slot in the chisel. It's a good idea when making deep cuts to retract the chisel frequently so waste won't clog in the cavity.

Always lock the hold-down so it rests on top of the work. This is necessary so the work will stay put when you retract the chisel. Sometimes it's necessary to place a backup below the work to raise it so the hold-down will be effective (photo 4). This is also important when cutting a through mortise because the backup will be damaged, which is why the project provides for an easily replaceable insert.

Side mortises (photo 5), whether they're stopped or through, are done by allowing only part of the chisel to penetrate the edge of the work. To keep the work from moving and to prevent damage to the fence, a strip of wood is placed between the work and fence so that, in effect, the chisel is making a full cut.

VARIATIONS

Mortise-and-tenon joints aren't restricted to square stock. The square cavities can be formed on round stock, even into the corners of square components. What you need to do this, and what I've designed into the mortising bench, is the V-block jig shown in photo 6. The jig replaces the conventional fence arrangement, positioning the work in the correct position. Construction details for the jig are shown on page 55. The V-block itself can be made by beveling one edge of two pieces of 3½"-wide material to 45° or by sawing a V down the center of a piece that's 7" wide.

In either case, the V is attached centrally to the base component with glue and No. 9 × 1¾" flathead screws. The best way to shape the hold-down is to cut a piece of hardwood to overall size and then bore a 1" hole to form the end of the slot. Next, saw away the waste and, with the part on its side, make a cut to reduce the height of the fingers to ¾".

It's a good idea to make the checking gauge (a ¾" × 3" × 3" *square* block) so the jig can be positioned accurately on the benchtop, as demonstrated in

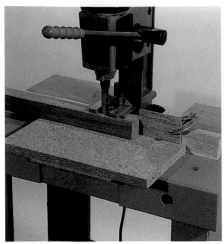

4 When cutting a traditional mortise, the hold-down should rest on the work, not be forced against it. Note the clamped stop block, in place to gauge the length of the mortise.

5 Side mortises are accomplished by placing a strip of wood between the work and the fence. The chisel cuts into both pieces. The extrawide fence is a wood facing that is attached to the regular fence. Holes in the fence provide for the addition.

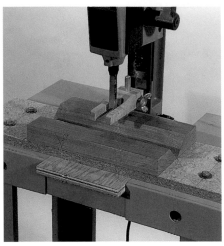

6 The V-block jig set up on the benchtop.

7 The gauge is used to accurately establish the position for the V-block jig. The text explains the procedure to follow.

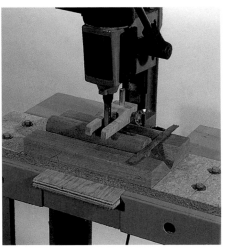

8 Mortising is done in a fairly routine fashion. The difference is that the work, cradled in a V-block, is round. A strip of wood, tack-nailed across the V, is used to gauge the length of the mortise.

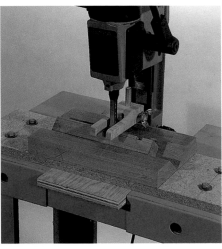

9 Mortising into the corner of square stock is also feasible. Start the cut very slowly to avoid allowing the bit to wander off the corner.

photo 7. After you've determined that the chisel is square to the fence, remove the fence and place the jig so the gauge is snug in the V while it "embraces" the chisel. Then, after locating the position of the attachment holes, drill ¹⁄₁₆" pilot holes through the jig's base and the benchtop. Enlarge the holes in the jig's base and in the benchtop to ½". The holes in the benchtop are for ⅜" threaded inserts. The base's holes, being ½", are a bit oversize for the ⅜" bolts that secure the jig, but this is to allow some "play" for

minor adjustments when the jig is mounted.

Operational procedures, feed pressure and such stay the same. The only change is the method used to position round work for accurate mortising (photo 8). To keep cuts consistent, mark a longitudinal line on the work that can be followed by the chisel. Radial mortises can be formed by using a stop block to keep the work in position while you rotate it for subsequent cuts. To picture the latter, imagine what you would have by removing a triangular

wedge from a round post so the square corner of a shelf can be inserted.

Mortising into corners of square stock is a basic procedure, except that slow feed is required when starting the cut to keep the bit from wandering before it is firmly seated (photo 9).

In all, the V-block technique advances square-hole operations beyond the basics of conventional mortising. I believe you'll spend lots of time using your mortiser and its stand, but not nearly as much time as you would have with a drill press attachment.

DIAGRAM 1A

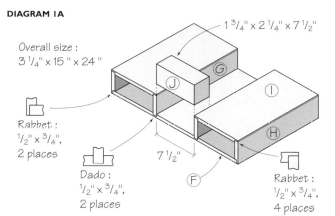

Overall size :
3 1/4" x 15 " x 24 "

1 3/4" x 2 1/4" x 7 1/2"

Rabbet :
1/2" x 3/4",
2 places

Dado :
1/2" x 3/4",
2 places

7 1/2"

Rabbet :
1/2" x 3/4",
4 places

DIAGRAM 1C

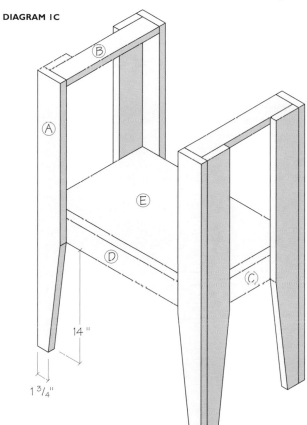

14 "

1 3/4"

Schedule of Materials: **MORTISING BENCH**

No.	Part	Item	Dimensions T W L	Material
1	F	Base	3/4" x 15" x 23 1/2"	Plywood
2	G	Partitions	3/4" x 2 3/4" x 15"	Lumber
2	H	Ends	3/4" x 3" x 15"	Lumber
2	I	Tops	3/4" x 8 1/4" x 15"	Plywood
1	J	Riser	1 3/4" x 2 1/4" x 7 1/2"	Hardwood

DIAGRAM 1B

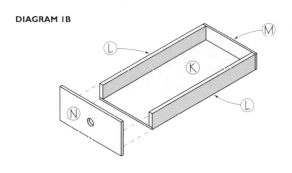

Schedule of Materials: **DRAWERS**

No.	Part	Item	Dimensions T W L	Material
2	K	Bottoms	1/4" x 6 3/4" x 12"	Plywood
4	L	Sides	3/4" x 1 1/2" x 12"	Lumber
2	M	Backs	1/4" x 1 3/4" x 6 3/4"	Plywood
2	N	Fronts	1/4" x 3 1/4" x 8 1/4"	Plywood

Schedule of Materials: **STAND**

No.	Part	Item	Dimensions T W L	Material
8	A	Legs	3/4" x 3" x 32"	Lumber
2	B	Braces	3/4" x 2 1/4" x 13"	Lumber
2	C	Rails	3/4" x 2 1/2" x 13"	Lumber
2	D	Rails	3/4" x 2 1/2" x 19"	Lumber
1	E	Shelf	3/4" x 13" x 20 1/2"	Plywood

MORTISE JIG

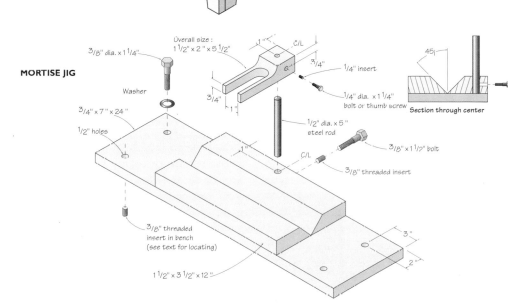

3/8" dia. x 1 1/4"

Washer

3/4" x 7 " x 24 "

1/2" holes

Overall size :
1 1/2" x 2 " x 5 1/2"

1"

C/L

3/4"

1/4" insert

1/4" dia. x 1 1/4"
bolt or thumb screw

3/4"

1"

1/2" dia. x 5 "
steel rod

1"

C/L

45°

Section through center

3/8" x 1 1/2" bolt

3/8" threaded insert

3/8" threaded
insert in bench
(see text for locating)

1 1/2" x 3 1/2" x 12"

3"

2"

A bench for the hollow chisel mortiser makes it a truly "independent" tool. The project requires little room and can be mounted on casters for easier mobility. Be sure that casters, if used, are the locking type.

This band saw is shown equipped with guides made by Carter Products Company. These guides reduce blade friction and increase cutting accuracy and blade life. They don't come cheap, however. Depending on your band saw, the guides can cost between $150 and $170.

Know your Band Saw

You'll cut circles around other saws

with these tune-up and technique tips.

The band saw can cut wood faster and deeper than any other sawing machine. I once observed a band saw at a mill that was one-story high, had a 12"-wide blade and was slicing through a 24" fir log like it was balsa. On a home-shop scale, this type of performance can even be accomplished with "small" band saws.

However, the machines you most often find in home shops are especially notable for cuts that require more finesse, such as following a curved line (photo 1) or resawing — which is the business of reducing the thickness of a board or producing a number of thinner boards from a single piece of thicker lumber (photo 2).

FUSSY AT FIRST

There are no secrets to correctly using a band saw, but it can be persnickety (more so than any other tool) when you neglect to align your blade. So "tuning" your saw is essential. First, with the machine unplugged, raise the blade guard and back off the blade guides and the thrust bearing (diagram 1). Open the wheel covers and lower the upper wheel (or whichever wheel is applicable for a three-wheeled saw) to relieve the tension enough so the mounted blade is easy to remove. Be sure the tires on the wheels are clean; I use a stiff-bristled toothbrush. Incidentally, the tires do wear down.

So if you see the crowns on the tires have flattened, it's time to replace them; otherwise your blade won't track properly.

Next, carefully mount the new blade and apply enough tension so the blade will stay put as you hand-turn the wheel. A good trick to keep your blade from falling off the top wheel during installation is to use a spring clamp or two to hold the blade to the top wheel as you increase the tension. While continuing to hand-turn the wheel, adjust the tracking until the blade stays centered on the wheel. Then adjust the tension to the setting suggested by the scale on the machine and, if necessary, fine-tune the tracking adjustment. Now close the wheel covers, turn on the tool for 30 seconds and then check your adjustments again.

Tensioning can be arbitrary. Many experienced band saw users consider the tension to be perfect when they can raise the guard to its highest point and can flex the blade about ⅛" with light finger pressure. And different cuts use different tension. I use a bit less tension when doing scroll saw–type work and a bit more when making straight cuts and when resawing.

Finally, adjust the blade guides and the thrust bearing. These should be close to the blade but not touching it when the blade is running free. How much clearance? The "gauge" I use for the blade guides is a still-crisp dollar bill. Locking the thrust bearing

about ¹⁄₆₄" away from the back edge is adequate.

BLADES

Most common styles of band saw blades are shown here (diagram 2). All these types are available in various widths and lengths that suit most band saws. Widths vary from ⅛" to 1" with a various number of teeth per inch. The more teeth, the smoother the cut. Thus, a narrow, fine-toothed blade is ideal for scroll saw–type work; a wide blade with fewer and coarser teeth is best for resawing. There are some exceptions to this, however. I often use a finer blade when sawing thick but soft wood because I want as smooth a cut as possible. In this case, you should feed the wood slowly, allowing the blade to cut at its own pace.

The width of the blade determines the radius it can turn. This is often listed as a specific figure, but the design of the blade is the determining factor, which is why diagram 3 shows some flexibility. A blade with a heavy set is able to turn tighter than a comparable blade with a very light set simply because the heavy blade makes a wider kerf, which allows more room for turning.

Unfortunately, band saw blades can have a fault called "lead." When you move stock into a blade, you expect the blade to follow the pattern line. When it doesn't (and you've correctly aligned your blade), the problem is

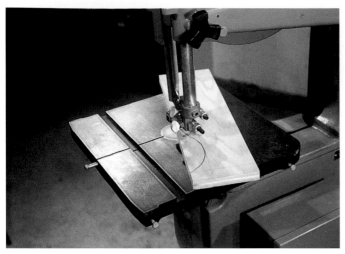

1 The band saw is notable for cutting curves in thin or thick stock. It saws fast, which often tempts us to rush the cut.

2 Resawing, the business of producing several thin boards from a thick one, is a band saw exclusive. The work can be guided by a fence, but the work will go smoothly only if the blade is in good condition. In general, when resawing, use the widest blade the machine can take.

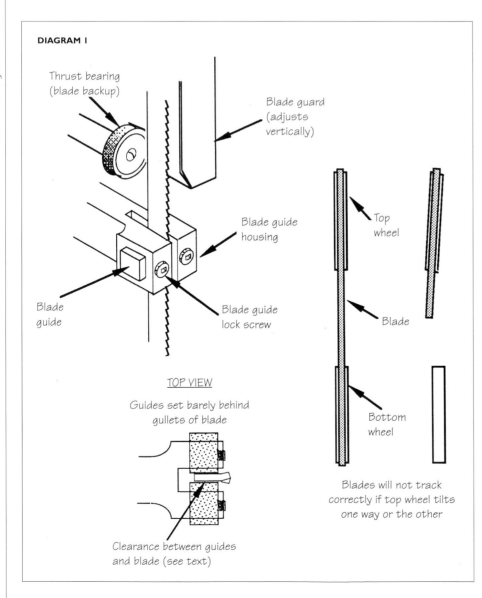

DIAGRAM I

Thrust bearing (blade backup)

Blade guard (adjusts vertically)

Blade guide housing

Blade guide

Blade guide lock screw

TOP VIEW

Guides set barely behind gullets of blade

Clearance between guides and blade (see text)

Top wheel

Blade

Bottom wheel

Blades will not track correctly if top wheel tilts one way or the other

likely a blade that is sharper on one edge. As a result, the blade "leads" off toward its sharper side. One solution is to compensate as you feed the stock. Experienced operators will correct a slight lead by backing up the blade with a piece of softwood and using a fine stone to hone the errant side. It's a negative approach because its purpose is to bring both sides of the blade to equal dullness. However, it extends the life of the blade.

Speaking of extending blade life, there are two ways to keep your blades cutting longer. First, substitute "slippery" blade guides if your saw is equipped with ordinary steel ones. These cool-running guides made from graphite or resin can be found in most tool catalogs, and they greatly reduce the friction between the guides and the blade. Second, lubricate the blade, but not with oil or wax. Instead, use a spray-on kitchen shortening. This will lead to smoother sawing and longer blade life and will cut down on noise.

When you're not working at the band saw, take the tension off the blade. Blades get warm from cutting and can shrink or stretch. If you leave the blade tightened, it can distort or flatten the crowns of your tires and strain the tool's bearings and shafts.

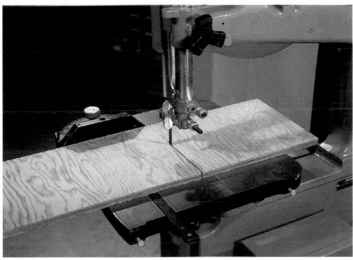

3 Check to make sure your blade and table slot are parallel by first crosscutting a wide piece of stock. Check the cut with a square. Also, use the cut pieces as a gauge to check that the blade is cutting square to the table.

Timber Wolf II & III

There have been innovations in saw blade design (different tooth styles, methods of hardening), but the Timber Wolf blades were the first to combine "thin kerf" and "low tension." This is an excellent combination because a thin kerf means smoother cuts, and low tension means your blades last longer.

With many blades, a thin kerf could mean you are going to have a hard time sawing tight turns. Not with these blades. They are heat-treated in the front and back so the middle area is "soft." In essence, they bend or cup around a turn so they can actually saw a smaller radius than a conventional blade.

As a test, I did some sawing without setting the blade guides or thrust bearing. And I raised the guard higher than it should have been. Of course, this is not the way you should work, but I wanted to see what happened. I didn't force the wood through, and I was impressed when the blade kept tracking as it should.

The blades have milled teeth made of Swedish silicon carbonite, a tough material that doesn't heat up as much as conventional steel — so the chance of burn marks is greatly reduced. The blades come with special instructions for a low-tension setup.

The manufacturer says the blades will last three to four times as long as conventional blades. I wasn't able to verify that, but from what I saw, I could be a believer.

Available from

SUFFOLK MACHINERY CORP.
12 Waverly Ave.
Patchogue, NY 11772
800-234-7297, www.timberwolf1.com

PS WOOD MACHINES
10 Downing St., Suite 3
South Park, PA 15129
800-939-4414, www.pswood.com

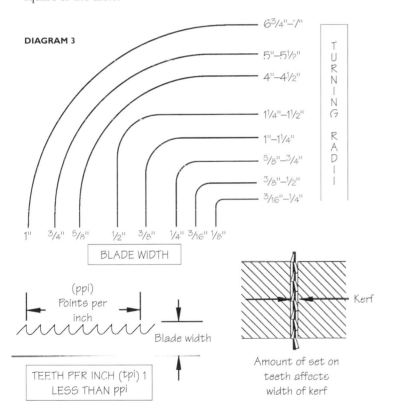

DIAGRAM 3

TURNING RADII

6³/₄"–7"
5"–5¹/₂"
4"–4¹/₂"
1¹/₄"–1¹/₂"
1"–1¹/₄"
⁵/₈"–³/₄"
³/₈"–¹/₂"
³/₁₆"–¹/₄"

1" ³/₄" ⁵/₈" ¹/₂" ³/₈" ¹/₄" ³/₁₆" ¹/₈"

BLADE WIDTH

(ppi) Points per inch

Blade width

TEETH PER INCH (tpi) 1 LESS THAN ppi

Kerf

Amount of set on teeth affects width of kerf

DIAGRAM 2

A regular or "standard" blade is usually supplied with machine. It makes smooth cuts and is a good bet for thin materials. In narrow width, it does acceptable scroll saw–type cutting.
Good assortment =
⅛" × 14 tpi, ³/₁₆" × 10 tpi

The skip tooth blade has wider tooth spacing for greater chip clearance to help prevent clogging. It cuts faster than a regular blade in thick material and when resawing.
Good choice = ³/₈" × 4 tpi

The hook tooth blade has a positive rake angle (teeth angle forward). It cuts aggressively and is a good choice for thick wood and hardwoods.
Good choice = ⅛" × 4 tpi

To make sure the blade and table slot are parallel, use a miter gauge to crosscut a wide piece of stock and then check the cut with a square (photo 3). To check the angle between the table and the blade, flip one of the cut pieces and put the two cut ends together. They should mate perfectly. If they don't, adjust the table so the angle between its surface and the side of the blade is 90°.

WHEN WORKING

One of the strengths of the band saw — fast cutting — can also be a fault. Not of the machine's, but of the operator's. We all tend to rush our cuts without paying enough attention to wood density, grain structure and the intricacy of the cuts. So it's always necessary to carefully guide the work and let the blade cut at its own pace.

Some thoughts on good cutting

techniques are shown in diagram 4. Plan your cuts to minimize the amount of backtracking you have to do. To avoid getting "trapped" because of the machine's column, preview the cut before sawing. Determining the best start point (diagram 5) helps you avoid complications.

Straight sawing against a fence works well as long as the blade is in good condition (photo 4). I use the simple fence in diagram 6 for both ripping and resawing. Resawing, in addition to creating many thin boards from a thick one, is also a good way to make identical parts from a single block. First cut the stock to the desired shape. Then slice off the pieces (photo 5).

There are many jigs that can be made for a band saw. One that I really appreciate is the V-block jig shown being used in photo 6 and that is detailed in diagram 7. With this jig you can find the center of stock that is to be mounted in a lathe by making slight intersecting cuts at each end of the material.

No article about band saws would be complete without some mention of compound sawing. This technique allows you to make a Queen Anne cabriole leg. The first step is to be sure the parent stock is square. Use a cardboard pattern to mark the profile on adjacent sides of the wood (diagram 8). Start sawing by following the profile on one side of the stock. Plan your cuts so there are as few pieces of waste as possible. Next, reattach the waste pieces with tape. Then saw the second side. After this, the waste pieces will fall away to reveal the shape of the leg. Much like a sculptor, you use this trick to find the envisioned form that was hidden in the wood.

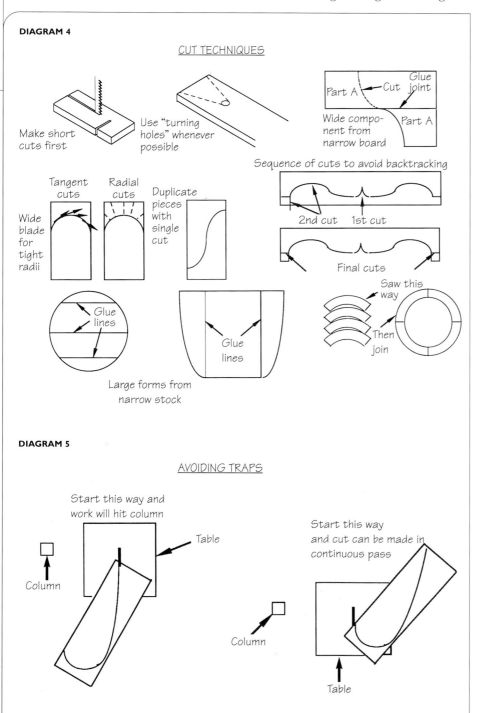

DIAGRAM 4

CUT TECHNIQUES

Make short cuts first

Use "turning holes" whenever possible

Part A — Cut — Glue joint

Wide component from narrow board — Part A

Tangent cuts

Radial cuts

Wide blade for tight radii

Duplicate pieces with single cut

Sequence of cuts to avoid backtracking

2nd cut   1st cut

Final cuts

Glue lines

Glue lines

Large forms from narrow stock

Saw this way

Then join

DIAGRAM 5

AVOIDING TRAPS

Start this way and work will hit column

Table

Column

Start this way and cut can be made in continuous pass

Column

Table

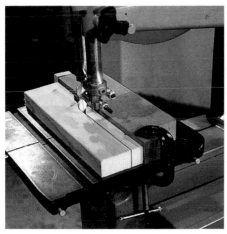

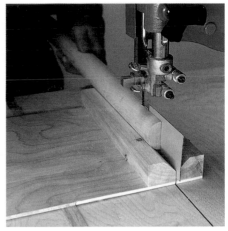

4 Simple ripping can also be done using a fence as a guide. Use a push stick to get work past the blade when there isn't enough room for your hands.

5 Resawing stock that has been cut to profile is the way to produce multiple identical pieces.

6 The V-block jig makes it easy to accurately halve or quarter round or square stock. The sheet-metal guide ensures that the work won't rotate as you move it forward.

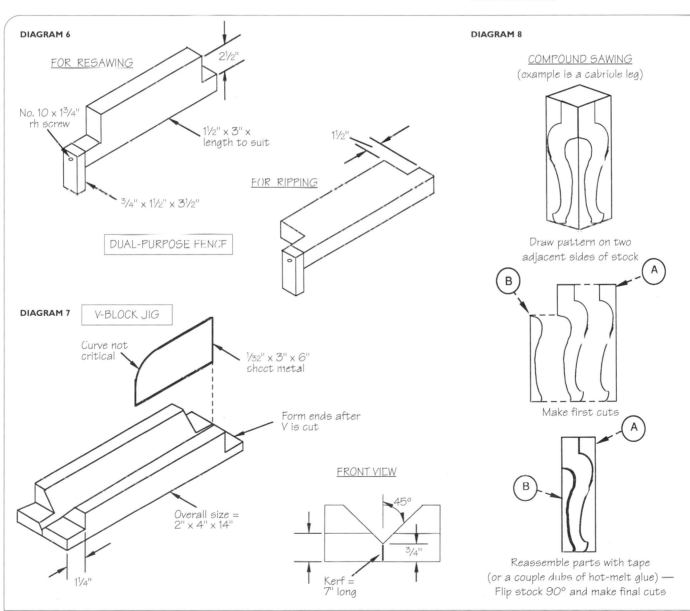

DIAGRAM 6

FOR RESAWING

2½"

No. 10 x 1¾" rh screw

1½" x 3" x length to suit

¾" x 1½" x 3½"

DUAL-PURPOSE FENCE

1½"

FOR RIPPING

DIAGRAM 8

COMPOUND SAWING
(example is a cabriole leg)

Draw pattern on two adjacent sides of stock

B   A

Make first cuts

A

B

Reassemble parts with tape
(or a couple dabs of hot-melt glue) —
Flip stock 90° and make final cuts

DIAGRAM 7   V-BLOCK JIG

Curve not critical

1/32" x 3" x 6" sheet metal

Form ends after V is cut

Overall size = 2" x 4" x 14"

1¼"

FRONT VIEW

45°

¾"

Kerf = 7" long

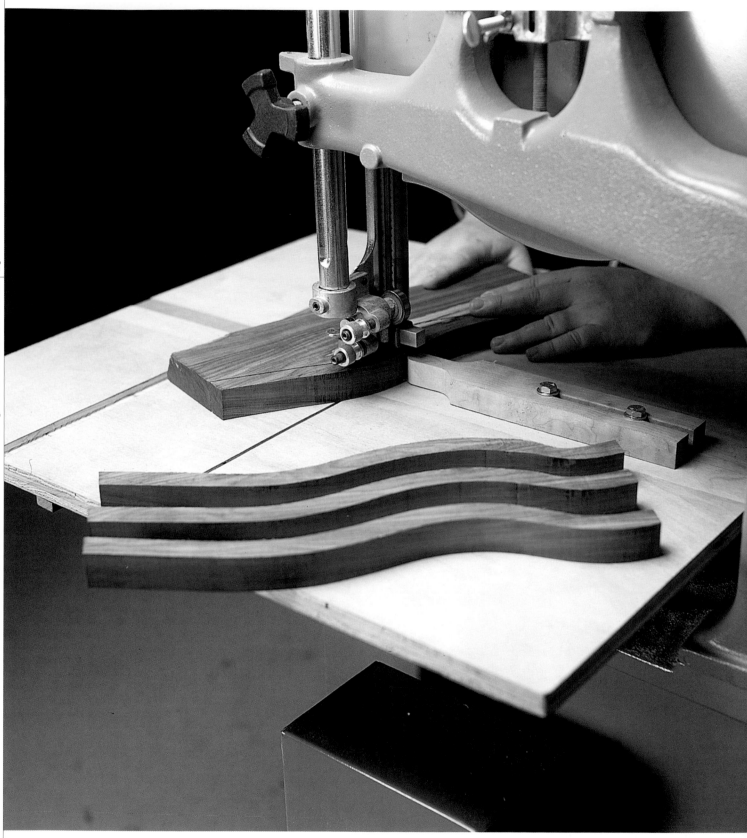

Band Saw Master Jig

This versatile and inexpensive jig is guaranteed to spiff up your saw.

If you use the band saw merely for freehand sawing of curved components and an occasional resaw chore, you're selling short one of your shop's most versatile machines. Just adding an oversize table will improve your work. Add accessories to that table, and you can split cylinders or turnings, saw parallel curves, saw patterns, cut accurate circles and crosscut round stock. Tricked out, the band saw gains the status it deserves.

My master jig was designed for the average "small" machine. If your unit has a 12" to 14" cutting capacity from the blade to the post and your table measures about 12" to 14" square, you should be able to make my jig with a few alterations.

Before building this jig, check two things on your saw. With the trunnion at 0, make sure the angle between the saw blade and the table is 90°. Also, verify the saw blade and the miter-gauge slot are parallel.

START WITH THE TABLE

Cut a piece of cabinet-grade plywood for the jig's table to size for your saw, then use the table saw to form the ⅛" kerf for the blade (see "The Table" diagram on page 64). Next, form the T-slot for the pivot slide centered on the table. Cut the 1" × 9" slot using your table saw to define the width of the slot (stop short of the final length). Extend the cuts with a handsaw. Remove the

waste with a chisel. Now widen the bottom half of the slot to 2" with a dado or by repeated passes with a saw blade. The cuts make ⅜"-deep by ½"-wide rabbets (detail A).

Next, use your table saw to cut the slot for the miter gauge. Locate it 6" away from the outside edge of the table. Its depth and width must match the bar of your miter gauge.

Drill holes for the three ⁵⁄₁₆" threaded inserts as shown; install them through the bottom of the table until they are almost flush with the table's surface.

TABLE GUIDE

On the underside of the table, attach a table guide (B) that slides in the machine's miter slot. Here's how: Put the table guide in the saw's miter slot, then position the jig's table so its right edge and the guide are parallel. Secure the guide by tacking through the table, then attach the guide permanently with four No. 4 × ¾" fh screws from the bottom of the guide and glue. Drill shank and pilot holes for the screws so they won't split or spread the guide when installed.

ADD THE BRACES

Prepare the part for the fence brace (F) and then cut the ½" × ¾" rabbet. Attach the brace to the table with glue and 4d finishing nails. Now cut the table brace (C) to size and install the ¼" threaded insert as shown, then glue and clamp the brace in place until the glue sets.

TABLE LOCKS AND TIE

Use aluminum angle with 1¼" legs for the table locks. Because some pivot-guided work requires good alignment between blade teeth and pivot point, a slot in the top leg of the angle is needed. This allows the jig's table to be moved to allow for blade width and tracking adjustment.

Drill holes through the vertical leg of the locks to match the holes that are in the table for adding aftermarket accessories. Use bolts to secure the locks to the saw's table and put the jig's table in place. Use an awl to pierce the underside of the table at the front end of the slot in the lock and then install the ¾" rh screws.

Make the table tie from aluminum strap. Attach it to the underside of the table so it spans the kerf. The tie keeps the table level on both sides of the kerf.

THE PIVOT AND FILLER SLIDES

The filler slide (G) and pivot slide (H) have the same T-shaped cross section and dimensions, so a good procedure is to start with parent stock that is 25" long and cut pieces to length after rabbeting the edges of the material. When the filler slide is in place, you'll see that it runs across the miter-gauge groove in the jig's table. So mark the location of the groove on the slide and then notch it so it won't interfere when using a miter gauge.

Mark the locations of the three No. 8 × 32 tpi threaded inserts that are

the **table**

PLAN VIEW OF TABLE

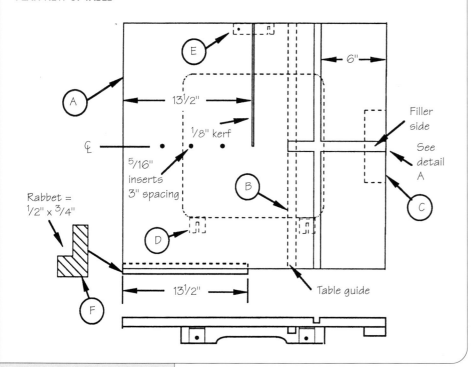

four No. 10 × 3" fh screws. Be sure to drill adequate shank and body holes and to countersink carefully before driving the screws. Before installing the front endpiece, carefully locate and drill the hole that is needed for the fence lock (K).

Now cut the fence lock to size, and accurately locate and drill the ¼" hole. Lay out the shape of the centered opening and saw away the waste with a band saw. Then use the band saw to shape the lock's edge profile but don't try to shape the rounded end exactly at this point. Instead, work by hand with sandpaper to dress the end so that, when the lock is pivoted down-ward, the rounded end will bear firmly against the fence brace to secure the fence's position.

ACCESSORIES

Cut material for the V-blocks (M and P) to size. Form the V-shaped trough by making a 45° bevel cut along one edge of stock that is 24" long and then halve the piece. For the parallel V-block, use glue and brads to attach the two pieces to the base so they form a V-trough.

Prepare the base (L) and attach it to the bottom of the block with glue and brads. Size the guide (N) so it will fit snugly in the table's miter-gauge slot. A little on the snug side is good so the accessory won't move.

To set up the parallel V-block, put the guide in place in the table groove

needed in the pivot slide. Install the in-serts so they're flush with the top sur-face of the slide. Make the pivot points by removing the head from No. 8 screws. Chuck one of them in a drill press and form a point with a file, or grip the screw in a portable drill and spin it against a turning grinding wheel.

MAKING THE FENCE

Cut stock for the fence body (I) to overall size. Shape the top edge on the band saw and smooth it with a drum sander. Next, cut the ends (J) to size and install the rear one with glue and

DETAIL A

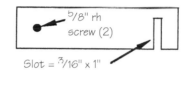

Rabbets = 3/8" x 1/2"

1"

1/4" x 1" thumbscrew

1/4" insert

Table brace 3/8" x 4" x 7"

TABLE TIE (PART E)

5/8" rh screw (2)

Slot = 3/16" x 1"

TABLE LOCK (PART D)

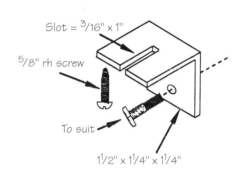

Slot = 3/16" x 1"

5/8" rh screw

To suit

1 1/2" x 1 1/4" x 1 1/4"

PIVOT SLIDE

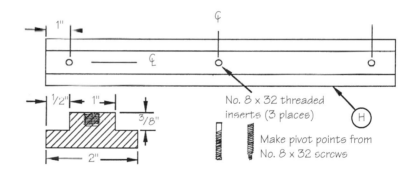

1"

1/2"   1"   3/8"

2"

No. 8 x 32 threaded inserts (3 places)

Ⓗ

Make pivot points from No. 8 x 32 screws

FILLER SLIDE

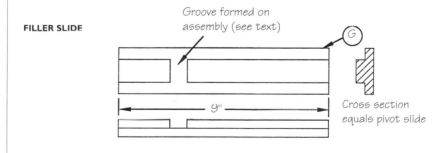

Groove formed on assembly (see text)

Ⓖ

9"

Cross section equals pivot slide

and position the block-base assembly so the cut path of the saw blade will be on the center of the V-cut. Mark the position of the guide and attach it to the underside of the base using glue and brads. Place the accessory in position and, with a fine saw blade mounted, saw a kerf about 6" long.

Make the splitter (O) by rounding off the top, forward edge and smoothing the edge. The splitter should fit tightly in the kerf. If not, cover the bottom edge with plastic tape to thicken it.

For the right-angle V-block, shape the guide (R) so it will ride smoothly in the table slot. Put the guide in the slot and position the V assembly (P and Q) so the angle between its forward edge and the side of the saw is 90°. Mark the position of the guide and then attach it to the block with glue and small nails.

TWO SAWING GUIDES

Shape the front ends of the guides (S and U) on the band saw and smooth the sawed edges with a drum sander. Drill a 3/16" end hole for the slot and saw out the waste. The guide is secured to the jig's table with 3/16" bolts that thread into the inserts installed in the table. The pattern-sawing guide is shaped like the one made for parallel curves except that the slot is shorter and the business end is notched to fit the saw blade that is used. The riser (T) is needed so the guide will be elevated above the workpiece.

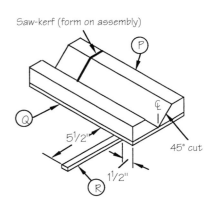

PARTS OF THE FENCE

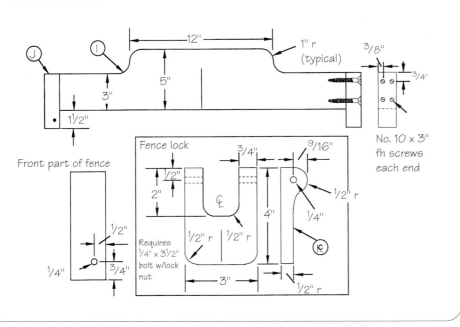

12"

1" r
(typical)

3/8"

3/4"

J

I

5"

3"

1 1/2"

No. 10 x 3"
fh screws
each end

Front part of fence

1/2"

1/4"

3/4"

Fence lock

1/2"

2"

3/4"

9/16"

℄

1/2" r

1/2" r

4"

1/4"

1/2" r

R

Requires
1/4" x 3 1/2"
bolt w/lock
nut

3"

1/2" r

the **V-blocks**

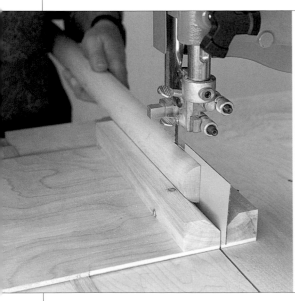

PARALLEL V-BLOCK

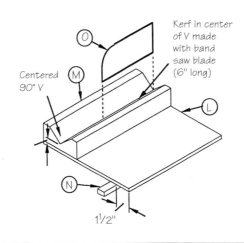

Kerf in center
of V made
with band
saw blade
(6" long)

Centered
90° V

O

M

L

N

1 1/2"

RIGHT-ANGLE V-BLOCK

Saw-kerf (form on assembly)

P

Q

℄

5 1/2"

1 1/2"

45° cut

R

the **guides**

PATTERN-SAWING GUIDE

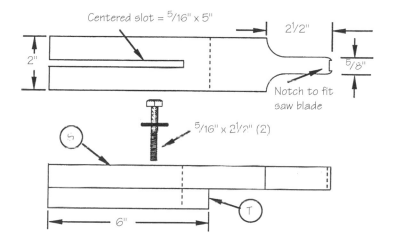

Centered slot = $^5/16$" x 5"

2"

$2^1/2$"

$^5/8$"

Notch to fit
saw blade

S

$^5/16$" x $2^1/2$" (2)

T

6"

PARALLEL CURVES GUIDE

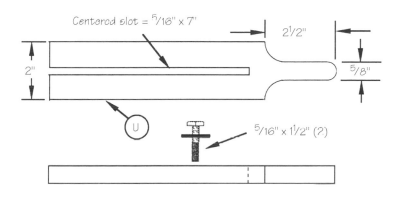

Centered slot = $^5/16$" x 7"

2"

$2^1/2$"

$^5/8$"

U

$^5/16$" x $1^1/2$" (2)

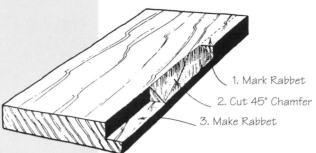

1. Mark Rabbet
2. Cut 45° Chamfer
3. Make Rabbet

tricks *of the* TRADE

ROUTING OAK

While making a display cabinet of oak and glass, I needed to cut ½" rabbets in the oak. In spite of my sharp router bit, I found myself splintering the oak. To avoid this, I first knocked off the sharp corners of the oak down to a depth equal to the rabbet (½") with a 45° chamfer cutter. Then I went back over it to cut the rabbet and got no tear-out.

Kingsley Hammet, Santa Fe, NM

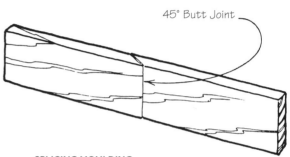

45° Butt Joint

SPLICING MOULDING

When butt-joining the ends of a continuous piece of moulding, such as baseboards, trim the ends at 45°. That way, the end of one board can overlap the end of the other so the joint will be less apparent if wood movement occurs.

Anne Westbrook Dominick, Hinsdale, New Hampshire

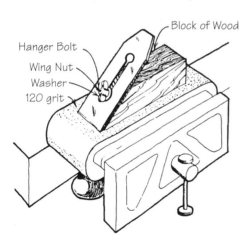

Block of Wood

Hanger Bolt
Wing Nut
Washer
120 grit

SHARPENING ON A BELT SANDER

If you don't have a bench grinder, here's a quick way to restore the bevel on a plane iron using a belt sander. Cut the end of a block of two-by at the proper angle for the bevel you need. Drill a ¼" hole perpendicular to this angled surface, and countersink the other side to accept the head of a ¼" carriage bolt.

Lock the iron in place with a washer and a wing nut, then make a few light passes on a belt sander (here is shown a portable model clamped upside down in a bench vise). Use a belt that is 120 grit or finer, then finish honing on oilstones.

W.K. Alexander, Richland, Washington

DOWEL TENONING JIG

Here's how I use my shaper to cut tenons on the ends of dowels that are to be used for chair rungs: I clamp to the fence a board that has a dado cut in it that is as wide and deep as the dowel's diameter. It should be at least twice as high as the length of the tenon. You may also need to add a wooden auxiliary fence for the cutter to bite into when set up in the proper position.

I grind the corner of the cutter to make a beveled shoulder, since square shoulders don't work well for most chair rungs.

Don Taylor, Deep River, Minnesota

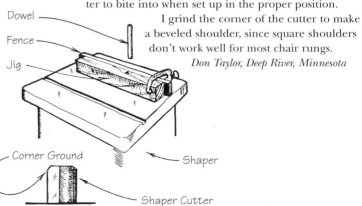

Dowel
Fence
Jig
Corner Ground
Shaper
Shaper Cutter

Head Stock

Lathe Bed

Tail Stock

Bolt

Nut

Spring

Locking Shoe

TAILSTOCK TIP

How many times have you gone to move your lathe's tailstock and had it jam when the metal locking shoe catches? I found a spring to fit over the bolt and between the bed and locking shoe. When you loosen the tailstock the spring expands, holding the shoe away from the bed so the assembly can slide easily.

Jerry Ernce, Broken Arrow, Oklahoma

COMPACT TABLE SAW SUPPORT

I didn't want to make space for a whole roller stand to support material coming off my table saw, so I came up with this small piece to use with my Black & Decker Workmate. By using ¾" ball-roller furniture glides instead of a roller, I can set this up lengthwise alongside the table saw to support material being crosscut. Install the roller glides into a length of 2×2 hardwood that has a groove cut in the bottom to receive a piece of ⅝" plywood. Size the plywood so that when it's placed on the cross-table supports of the Workmate, the top of the roller glides will be even with the top of the table saw.

Jay E. Wright, Chico, California

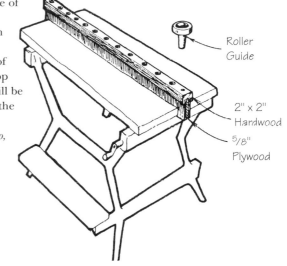

Roller Guide

2" x 2" Hardwood

⅝" Plywood

SQUARING ON A TABLE SAW

One of the biggest problems I have in my shop is squaring a large board that I've glued up from strips. Even with jointing, the two straight edges may not be exactly parallel, so you can't flip it over to reference the cut from both sides. I developed the following method to ensure a square board.

Use a framing square and mark one end of the board square to one side, and mark the edge you use as a guide. Measure the distance from the outside edge of the saw teeth and outside edge of the saw table (X). Place a square against the reference edge, and mark the distance (X) from the first line you marked.

Clamp a straightedge on the second line. (The clamps must be placed to the right of the straightedge.) Now flip the board over and let the straightedge butt against the right side of the saw tabletop. The straightedge and the tabletop will serve as a fence to guide the piece straight, and you will have excellent control. Do the same for the other end using the same reference edge.

Jan C. Plemmons, Jacksonville, Florida

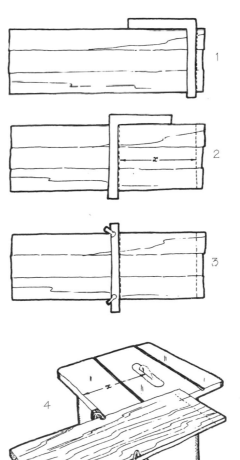

So You Say You Don't Have a Lathe

The gist of these thoughts is that it's possible to incorporate turnings in your projects even if you lack the lathe to form them or, on occasion, choose to take the easy way out. The skilled woodturner may scoff at the thought of buying ready-to-use lathe work, but you don't have to be a purist to be a good woodworker. Buying a component can be the answer to producing a project that's not otherwise feasible.

There are woodworkers who don't own a lathe and there are others, including myself, who do but won't hesitate to admit that while turning one piece is enjoyable and creative, having to clone components (such as four legs for a chair or table) is a production procedure to be tolerated without much enthusiasm, even if a duplicating accessory is available.

A fellow woodworker of my acquaintance takes another approach: Buy one leg and use it as a prototype to form the others. This eliminates the chore of having to design from scratch and is especially helpful when he's duplicating a piece of classic furniture.

Anyway, there is a cornucopia of ready-mades from which you can choose components. They range from an extensive collection of parts for toys and novelty projects, to sophisticated products like Queen Anne and William & Mary table legs. Also on tap

Here are Queen Anne carved legs from Matthew Burak Furniture *(above)*. These Country Sheraton legs also are from Matthew Burak Furniture *(left)*.

are cabriole-type legs that require both a band saw and a lathe to produce.

Matt Burak of Matthew Burak Furniture, a manufacturer of quality furniture that also produces top-grade furniture legs, says, "There's a niche for my legs in the hobbyist/small shop marketplace. The concept was simple. Supply a well-detailed and market-

proven selection of legs in different styles to people who are uninterested or unable to turn out a set of their own." Burak's company started with 8 leg styles in two wood species and is now offering 16 leg styles in five wood species. The legs are mortised and ready for assembly. Matching aprons and stretchers are also available.

AVAILABILITY

It's possible to find small parts (for toys and such) in hobby shops, and a variety of newels and balusters for stair work in good-size or specialty lumberyards. But generally, ready-mades is a mail-order business. The most extensive collections are available directly from the manufacturers or via catalogs. (See source list.)

HOW ABOUT COST?

Overall, the cost of a finished piece compared with buying the raw material is not prohibitive, especially when you consider the time, effort and expertise required to produce some of the products. In the small parts area, car and truck wheels for example, the cost is almost insignificant. Checking current catalogs, I noted the following prices:

A set of four 2¼" spoked wheels in maple costs $5.25. Typically, if you buy in quantity, the cost is reduced. In this case, buying 10-plus sets brings the price down to $3.75 per set.

In the leg category, prices relate to the complexity of the design. A carved cherry Queen Anne leg with a carved knee for a dining table lists for $62. A turned cherry Queen Anne leg, whose shape is essentially a taper that ends in a pad foot, is $39. William & Mary legs for a coffee table list at $19.50 in cherry, $18.50 in maple.

Regarding raw materials, when working from scratch, I figure turning squares usually fall in the 4×4 and 2×2 range depending on the design. Again quoting from current catalogs, 4×4s in cherry are about $22 a lineal foot; 2×2s about $3.50. Prices relate to wood species, with walnut being up there around $25 per lineal foot for 4×4s and about $4 for 2×2s. Note: These prices are a catalog average. Prices from your lumberyard may differ.

So we have choices. If you're interested, the best bet is to check the sources of supply and write or phone for information or catalogs. If you're an enthusiastic turner you'll ignore these options, but I have a feeling there are readers who will explore the possibilities.

source list

ADAMS WOOD PRODUCTS LTD.
974 Forest Dr.
Morristown, TN 37814
423-587-2942
www.adamswoodproducts.com

CLASSIC DESIGNS
BY MATTHEW BURAK
P.O. Box 329
St. Johnsbury, VT 05819
800-843-7405, www.tablelegs.com

TATRO, INC.
7011 Marcelle St.
Paramount, CA 90723
800-748-5827

BEAR WOODS SUPPLY CO., INC.
139 Bonaventure St.
Cornwallis, Nova Scotia
Canada B0S 1H0
800-565-5066,
www.bearwood.com

KLOCKIT (GENEVA SPECIALTIES)
P.O. Box 636, N3211 County Rd. H
Lake Geneva, WI 53147
800-556-2548, www.klockit.com

CONSTANTINE'S
2050 Eastchester Rd.
Bronx, NY 10461-2297
800-223-8087, www.constantines.com

WOODWORKER'S SUPPLY
1108 N. Glen Rd.
Casper, WY 82601
800-645-9292

WOODCRAFT
P.O. Box 1686, 5300 Briscoe Rd.
Parkersburg, WV 26102-1686
800-225-1153, www.woodcraft.com

CHERRY TREE
P.O. Box 369
Belmont, OH 43718
800-848-4363,
www.cherrytree-online.com

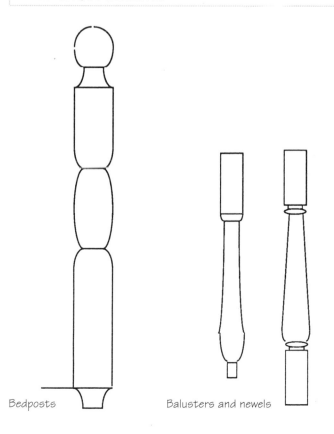

Bedposts   Balusters and newels

Mistakes happen all the time, even to the most experienced woodworkers. Putting a drawer side in backwards is an easy mistake to make, as you can see here.

Mistakes of the Hand and Mind

Arrgh! Another stupid mistake. Don't worry — try these handy tips and start nipping costly errors in the bud!

One of my recent projects was a book with the working title *Woodworking Mistakes and Solutions*. The job has opened a can of worms — or termites, as the case may be. I've run across statements like, "Expertise in woodworking is gained through trial and error," and, "Becoming a good woodworker is a matter of learning from mistakes." Granted, there is a human error factor, but your accepting the inevitability of error may be the biggest mistake of all.

While "playing" can be an enjoyable aspect of woodworking, step-by-step experimentation through a project can waste a lot of time — and material. My thought, though not an original one, is that we gain knowledge by going to school. In essence, going to school means we learn from the mistakes of others so we can avoid those errors. I see nothing wrong with our stating proudly, "I taught myself," but we shouldn't be overcome by it. If we had to learn everything on our own we'd probably still be counting on our fingers.

I received a letter from a 75-year-young lady, recently widowed, who thought that woodworking would help her through a bad period and beyond. "I was so frustrated," she wrote, "and then, thank goodness, I found one of your books in a local library. If I'd had to learn on my own I would have quit before putting up my first shelf."

I see two phases of woodworking: engineering, which deals with cutting and joining; and creativity, which deals with design and appearance, to which we react subjectively. We can design from scratch or work from plans offered by others, making changes that please our own senses. In engineering, there is rarely room for compromise. You can't stretch a board that's cut too short or widen one ripped too narrow. There are acceptable variables with many joints, but it's essential that components mate precisely.

Mistakes of the mind occur when we neglect to give woodworking proper attention. One of my recent projects was a small storage box I wanted for storing CD-ROM cases. The cases were to slide in grooves cut into opposite sides of the storage box. All went well through the material sizing and dadoing stages. I did the assembly and set the project aside to allow the glue to set. I even got to doing final sanding before I became aware of the goof that's shown in figure 1. Always do dry runs before the final step.

I've wondered more times than I care to admit why a board seems shorter or, say, narrower than my measurements intended them to be. Being preoccupied may cause you to overlook important details — remember, saw blades have a "right" and a "wrong" side (figure 2). Unless you

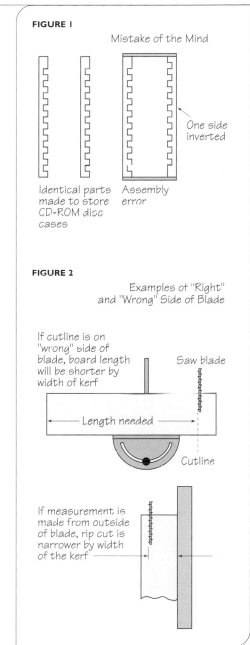

FIGURE 1

Mistake of the Mind

Identical parts made to store CD-ROM disc cases

Assembly error

One side inverted

FIGURE 2

Examples of "Right" and "Wrong" Side of Blade

If cutline is on "wrong" side of blade, board length will be shorter by width of kerf

Saw blade

Length needed

Cutline

If measurement is made from outside of blade, rip cut is narrower by width of the kerf

"I see nothing wrong with our stating proudly, 'I taught myself,' but we shouldn't be overcome by it. If we had to learn everything on our own we'd probably still be counting on our fingers."

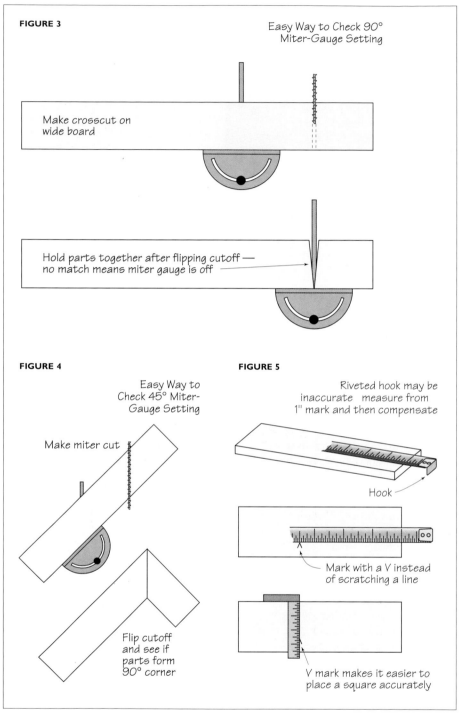

FIGURE 3

Easy Way to Check 90° Miter-Gauge Setting

Make crosscut on wide board

Hold parts together after flipping cutoff — no match means miter gauge is off

FIGURE 4

Easy Way to Check 45° Miter-Gauge Setting

Make miter cut

Flip cutoff and see if parts form 90° corner

FIGURE 5

Riveted hook may be inaccurate   measure from 1" mark and then compensate

Hook

Mark with a V instead of scratching a line

V mark makes it easier to place a square accurately

make sure the cut is on the waste side of the dimension line, you will reduce width, or length, by the gauge of the blade. This kind of mistake prompted the adage "measure twice, cut once." There's another factor to measuring twice. It slows you a bit, helping to induce a pace that's conducive to accurate and more pleasurable woodworking — like occasionally taking a deep breath.

We know how important it is for

tool components to be in alignment, but we do it once and then forget that there are factors, like vibration, that can thwart us. It would be excessive to check daily, but there are ways to prove accuracy as you go. For example, when crosscutting on a table saw, flip the cutoff and butt it against the part from which it was cut (figure 3). If they don't match, check the miter gauge. This test will also alert you when the angle between the blade and

FIGURE 6

Hold ruler at an angle — slide marker down graduation

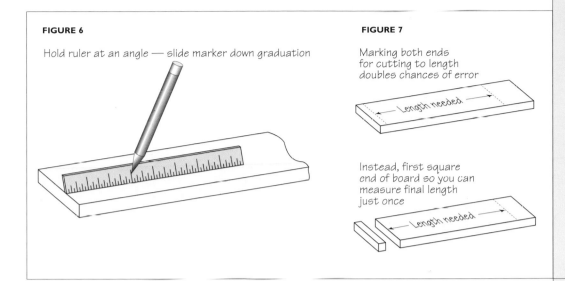

FIGURE 7

Marking both ends
for cutting to length
doubles chances of error

Length needed

Instead, first square
end of board so you can
measure final length
just once

Length needed

table is not 90°. The thought also applies when sawing 45° miters. You'll know attention to alignment is required if the flipped cutoff and the parent piece do not form a 90° corner (figure 4). Like many of us, I do a lot of measuring with a flex tape, but I don't always trust the hook, regardless of whether it swivels or slides. When I need to be more careful, I measure from the 1" mark (and remember to add the inch so my work won't be shorter than I intend). I mark an inverted V instead of scratching a dimension point. This makes it easier, for example, to place a square accurately (figure 5). When using a steel rule it's a good idea to hold it at an angle and slide the marker down a graduation line, which is more accurate than placing the rule flat and scratching a line (figure 6).

Often, when sawing a board to length, we mark the length "in the field" to be sure the board will have square ends. A better method is to square one end first then measure for length. This will reduce your chances of measuring and sawing errors (figure 7).

I've come to accept, as we all should, that lumber and plywood thicknesses have plus-or-minus tolerances. This becomes apparent, and frustrating, when you've cut a groove with a dado assembly and discover that the insert piece is too thick or too thin to fit correctly. We can't fatten or put the material on a diet, so we compensate by using shims of various gauges.

FIGURE 8   Dado-Width Gauge

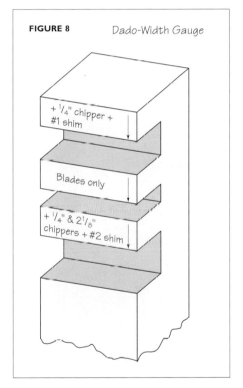

+ $\frac{1}{4}$" chipper +
#1 shim

Blades only

+ $\frac{1}{4}$" & $2\frac{1}{8}$"
chippers + #2 shim

To avoid having to make frequent test-cuts, I have a dado gauge like the one shown in figure 8. Each time I'm sure of the cut, I make one in the gauge and mark it to list the blades, chippers and shims that are needed. It saves a lot of time, eliminates trial and error, and certainly contributes to accuracy.

If we work carefully, with full attention to the job at hand, we adopt methods that contribute to expertise while minimizing if not eliminating errors. These practices should be part and parcel of our everyday life in the woodshop.

"While 'playing' can be an enjoyable aspect of woodworking, step-by-step experimentation through a project can waste a lot of time — and material."

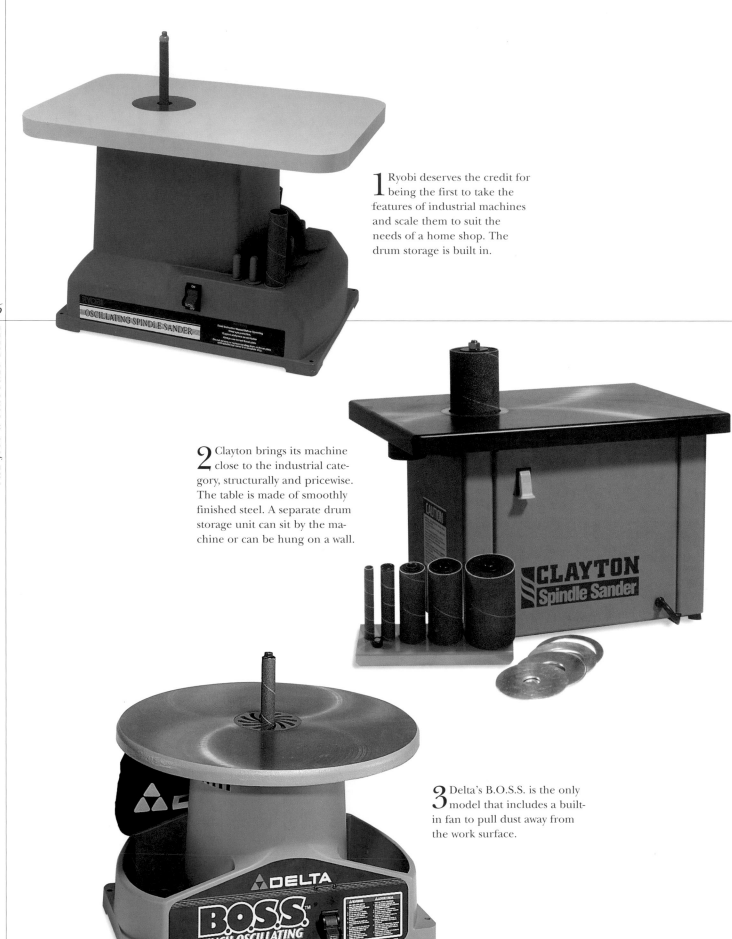

1 Ryobi deserves the credit for being the first to take the features of industrial machines and scale them to suit the needs of a home shop. The drum storage is built in.

2 Clayton brings its machine close to the industrial category, structurally and pricewise. The table is made of smoothly finished steel. A separate drum storage unit can sit by the machine or can be hung on a wall.

3 Delta's B.O.S.S. is the only model that includes a built-in fan to pull dust away from the work surface.

Oscillating Spindle Sanders

Modern units oscillate vertically as they spin, revolutionizing home-shop spindle sanding.

Every so often a new tool comes along that supplants what had become the traditional way of accomplishing a woodworking chore. The independent hollow chisel mortiser discussed in "Put the Mortiser to Work" on page 52 affected the drill press's role as a mortising machine. Now oscillating spindle sanders are beating out the drill press for drum sanding by being ready instantly for use. In fact, industrial shops have been using "big brother" versions of the sanders for decades.

It still would be unworthy to disregard drill press drum sanding. I've used the system too long to be so disloyal. Yet it's nice to eliminate its negative factors, such as possible wood burn, short sleeve life and rapid heat buildup, without relying on finesse and the need for a special table to allow the drum to move vertically.

Oscillating spindle sanders cut more aggressively than single-action drums. This is because the dual action constantly changes the abrasive area that contacts the work's edge, thus reducing the need for feed pressure. This leads to better control over stock removal, increasing the guarantee that the sanded edge will be square to adjacent surfaces.

The additional drum action truly minimizes the tendency of abrasive grits to become clogged with dust. A

single action drum "scores" horizontal lines in the wood, whereas the abrasive grains of a drum that oscillates cut in a random pattern to produce smoother results. The motion resembles the action of portable, random-orbit pad sanders.

WHAT'S OUT THERE?
Many units are available, with a lot of them falling in the industrial range. I

4 The Ridgid model is a convenient combination machine that offers toolless conversion from belt to spindle. Lightweight, it has built-in carrying handles, a bevelling table and a sawdust collection port.

specifications

COMPANY	RYOBI	CLAYTON	RIDGID	DELTA
Model	OSS450	140	EB4424	B.O.S.S.
Motor	Universal (3.5 amps)	Induction ½ hp	Induction ⅜ hp (4.6 amps)	Induction ¼ hp
Spindle rpm	2,000	1,750	1,725	1,725
Strokes	58	58	60	60
Spindle diameter	½"	½"	½"	½"
Spindle stroke	⅝"	¹³⁄₁₆"	¾"	⅞"
Spindle length	4½"	4½"	4½"	4½"
Abrasive sleeves	½", 1"	½", ¾", 2", 3"	½", 2"	½", ¾"
Optional sleeves	¾", 1½", 2", 3"	1", 1¼", 1½", 2¼", 2½"	¾", 1", 1½", 3"	1", 1½", 2", 3"
Table size	14" x 20"	13¾" x 21"	20" x 20"	18" dia.
Table material	Laminated MDF	Ground steel	Cast aluminum	Cast iron
Dust collection	Yes	Yes	Yes	Yes
Storage rack	Yes	Yes	Yes	Yes
Weight	28 lbs.	80 lbs.	39 lbs.	41 lbs.
Retail price	$283	$638	$239	$199

settled on four models that pretty much run the gamut of machines that, functionally and pricewise, fill the needs of home and small commercial woodshops. The machines efficiently produce the multiple action that makes them unique, but differences exist in the mechanisms. The Ryobi and the Clayton (photos 1 and 2) employ similar systems. Both have belt-driven double pulleys at the base of the spindle shaft. The one that turns the spindle develops fewer revolutions per minute (rpm) than its companion. The difference, which varies depending on the design, moves the spindle up and down a certain number of times per minute because of an integral circular ramp. The Clayton's ramp mechanism is encased in an oil-filled housing, which suggests "heavy duty."

The Ridgid unit and the Delta B.O.S.S. (Bench Oscillating Spindle Sander) (photos 3 and 4) don't use drive belts. The Ridgid unit functions with an eccentric that, while secured to the motor shaft, drives a gear that's inside a grease-filled housing. A cam follower, actually a disc with upward extending pins on its perimeter, turns inside a ramp. In effect, the pins move up and down to transfer the action to the spindle.

The B.O.S.S. has a simple oscillat-

DIAGRAM 1 AUXILIARY TABLE

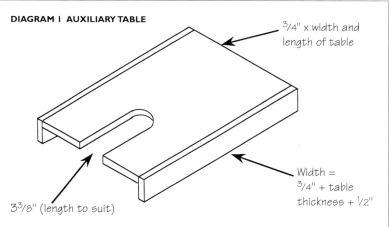

¾" x width and length of table

Width = ¾" + table thickness + ½"

3⅜" (length to suit)

An auxiliary table is a wise addition for any machine. It slips easily on or off and can be clamped in place when necessary.

DIAGRAM 2 PIVOT SANDING JIG

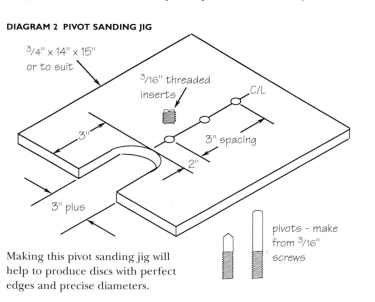

¾" x 14" x 15" or to suit

³⁄₁₆" threaded inserts

C/L

3"

3" spacing

2"

3" plus

pivots - make from ³⁄₁₆" screws

Making this pivot sanding jig will help to produce discs with perfect edges and precise diameters.

ing system, whereby the lower end of the motor shaft drives a worm gear that rotates a cross shaft. It uses two eccentric cams to pull the entire motor/spindle assembly up and down.

Both the Delta and Ridgid units oscillate 60 times a minute at 1,725 rpm drum rotation.

All units have dust collection ports that connect nicely to a standard shop vacuum hose. The Delta model has a built-in suction fan to pull the dust into a collection bag, which offers a nice alternative to hooking up the shop vac.

I found that dust collection averaged better than 90 percent, which is pretty good but not perfect. Therefore, good maintenance involves occasionally using a small brush to dislodge stubborn debris that collects in the duct area under the spindle.

For specifications of the models discussed, refer to the Specifications chart.

GETTING THE MOST FROM ABRASIVE SLEEVES

Despite the oscillating action, normal sanding still uses only part of the abrasive surface. To maximize usage, change the work to contact area as frequently as needed. Do this by elevating the work on a piece of wood or plywood so a fresh area of abrasive becomes available. By duplicating the procedure after inverting the sleeve on the drum, you'll get as much usage as possible from an abrasive sleeve.

While using any handy piece of wood as an "elevator" is an option, it's better to make your own auxiliary table that's just right for your machine (diagram 1). It has the advantage that the accessory won't move and spoil your accuracy while you work.

MAKING A PIVOT JIG

Pivot jigs make it easy to produce perfect discs. I've made them for disc and belt sanders, but they're even more efficient for an oscillating drum sander (diagram 2). The jig is simple — it's made from a piece of plywood or particleboard, sized to suit the machine,

5 The pivot-sanding jig is clamped in place such that it and the drum have a common center line.

6 By adjusting the center point pin, the jig can form many circle sizes.

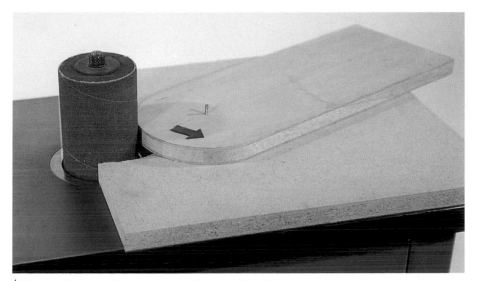

7 Again, the pivot jig proves useful for rounding the corners of the ends of boards.

and threaded inserts hold pivots made from ³⁄₁₆" screws (photos 5 and 6). Use the short, pointed pivot when the work doesn't have a center hole — the work is just impaled on the point. The longer one is suitable when a center hole is OK — say, for a wheel axle.

The same jig can be used to round off the ends of narrow, or even wide, stock (photo 7). If you'd like to experiment with the results, use the same setup but mount the work off center.

OTHER IDEAS

How do you produce the concave shape on, for example, the end of a rail that must fit a round leg? I've rejected my as-of-now methods for the dual-action drum sander method (photo 8). The bulk of the waste can be removed on a scroll saw or band saw, but if I don't get impatient, I can accomplish the whole job by sanding. If one of the drums that you have isn't suitable for the cove size needed, you can still use the idea by first rough-sawing, then finishing, with a drum that's smaller than the needed radius.

You also can reduce the width on the end of a component by using the setup shown in photo 9. Quite a bit of material can be removed in a single pass if you use a coarse abrasive. I can "cut" as deep as ³⁄₁₆", even with a relatively fine-grit sleeve, as long as I don't use force. In all situations, not using force has as much to do with preventing drum distortion and harm to the spindle as it does with getting quality results.

8 Producing a cove on the end of a piece works well, with a little patience.

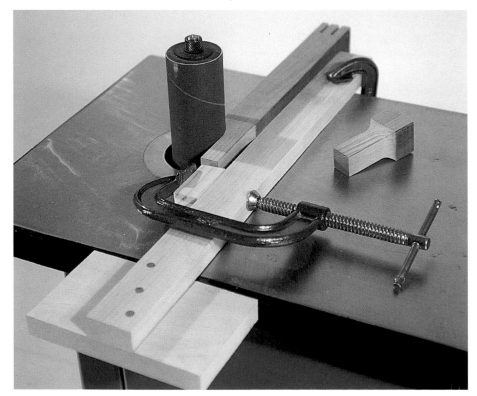

9 You can be quite generous with depth of cut to reduce width if you feed the work at a reasonable pace.

Making Sense of Router Bits

With so many options available, here's some help in deciding what's needed in your shop.

Few tools in recent years have made as strong an impact on woodworking as the electric router. This is especially true in the home shop where the tool can function like a mill shop. Mouldings, raised-panel doors, decorative edges, a variety of joints and more are now practical applications without needing a complement of stationary equipment.

This has led to a cornucopia of router tooling that can be bewildering, even intimidating, especially to the novice. Buying haphazardly is a bad approach, and suggesting that one needs all types is equally ill-advised. You don't have to buy too many quality bits before you exceed the price of the router itself. An informed background of router bit basics and the innovations available today can be helpful.

ANATOMY OF A ROUTER BIT

Router bits share common parts and traits (diagram 1). All bits have a shank, or shaft, most commonly found in ¼" and ½" diameters. The shank usually has two "wings" attached, which have the cutting edges milled onto them.

Most bits have pilots that guide the router and control the width of cut without a fence or edge guide. Pilots can be integral or replaceable ball bearings.

Integral pilots, usually found on one-piece bits, turn as fast as the cutting edges, creating considerable friction resulting in burns and indentations in the work if extreme care isn't used.

Pilot bearings, which are characteristic of tungsten carbide bits, rotate independently so the negative factors of the integral pilot are eliminated (diagram 1). "Field bits" do not have pilots so the router must be steered by an edge guide or by a straightedge that is clamped to the work (diagram 2).

Cutting radii is the distinguishing dimension on edging bits, many shaped bits and field bits. On straight bits, whose primary functions are dadoes, grooves and flush trimming, the full diameter size is used as the distinguishing dimension.

IN GENERAL

When all else is equal, choose carbide — the thicker the better — not only because of increased mass, but because thicker carbide cutters can be sharpened as many as 15 times while thinner high-speed steel ones will have to be replaced after about four or five sharpenings. There's a wide variety of choices in manufacturers' lines, so it pays to check around.

It seems foolish today to think of anything but carbide-tipped cutters, but they still haven't completely replaced all-steel tooling. You can save money by choosing from these lower-cost products if you need a bit for a

The shear angle of a bit is the angle that the cutting edge makes with the shank of the bit. The bit shown above employs carbide tips angled to slice through wood fibers, similar in principle to using a hand plane at an angle to the direction of motion. The slicing action becomes even more important when cutting cross-grain. Bits without shear or with too little shear chop the wood and are more likely to produce tearout and chatter marks. (Information provided by Freud.)

Here's a six-piece starter bit set from Freud.

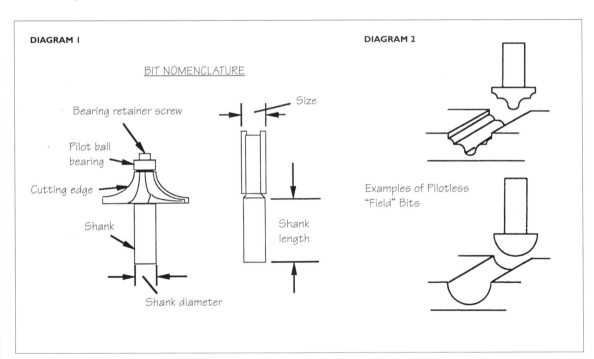

DIAGRAM 1

BIT NOMENCLATURE

Bearing retainer screw

Pilot ball bearing

Cutting edge

Shank

Size

Shank length

Shank diameter

DIAGRAM 2

Examples of Pilotless "Field" Bits

particular, short-use project. Generally though, acquiring high-quality bits is still the way to go.

MULTIPURPOSE BITS

Though most router bits are designed with a single function in mind (the rabbeting "kit" in diagram 3 includes an assortment of bearings, each of which establishes a specific width of cut), many can be utilized beyond their primary functions by controlling the width of cut and depth relative to the router base. For example, a straight bit (diagram 4) can form dadoes and grooves wider than its diameter by making repeat, overlapping passes.

Another flexible bit is the the multipurpose bit (diagram 5), which is configured so partial sections of it will produce standard profiles. By varying the cutter's height, fence position and number of passes, you can create a virtually unlimited number of moulding shapes.

Bits of this type must be used with a router table. By carefully checking what is available, it's often possible to buy one bit that can do the job of several others.

STARTER SET

Buying bits in sets is good advice costwise, but you must ask yourself if it's practical for your particular woodworking needs. A disadvantage to bit sets is that you may get more bits than your work or designs require. The answer is to avoid jumping into a purchase without checking the primary function of each bit and asking if there will be a need for each one (diagram 6).

If you're using your router for decorative edges, extensive joint forming, surface carving and so on, a set of bits may not be right for you because many sets include several profile bits and different-diameter straight bits. You may be happy to get along with only one type of each.

All sets are not alike, so check the contents against your woodworking application in order to make the most practical choice.

SAFETY BITS

The trend today is toward antikickback bits. The obvious difference between conventional bits and the newer designs is in bulk or mass. Instead of two wings supporting the cutting edges, antikickback bits are solid steel milled almost to the diameter of the cutting circle and with very narrow gullets. In essence, the design limits how deeply the cutting edge can bite into the wood and guards against wood being jammed too deeply into the gullets. I think extra mass also provides an advantage because more weight means less vibration.

Another safety factor has to do with vertical panel-raising bits that are 1" in diameter as opposed to those that work horizontally and have as much as a 3" cutting diameter. The smaller diameters of the vertical designs reduce tip and surface speeds considerably and require less horsepower. The bits are used in a router table with a high fence to support the work.

Some manufacturers add a colored coating to the bits so they show up more clearly, serving as a warning to keep fingers away. This adds a margin of safety to routing but raises an important purchasing question: Is the coating an antistick product that prevents accumulation of pitch and resin? If it's just a paint job, it will soon wear away, especially near cutting edges where the most heat is generated.

Talking safety about router bit design seems a bit much, but let's concede there is no such thing as safety overkill.

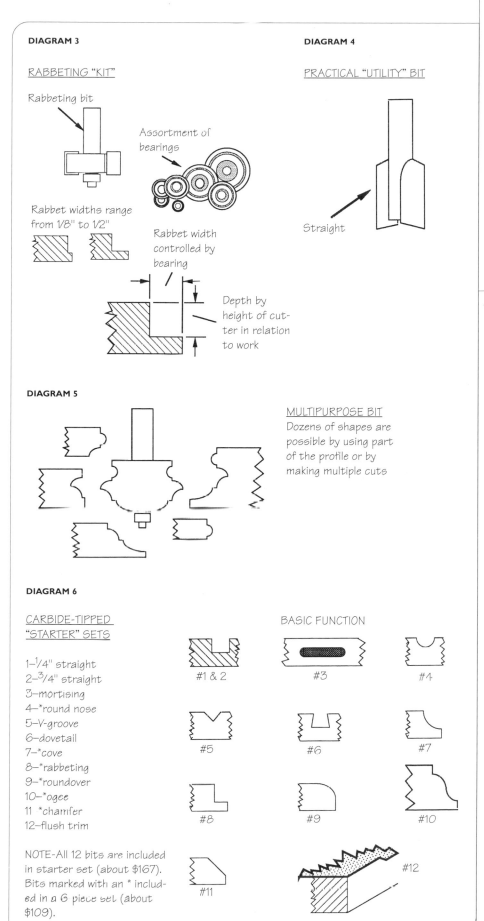

DIAGRAM 3

RABBETING "KIT"

Rabbeting bit

Assortment of bearings

Rabbet widths range from 1/8" to 1/2"

Rabbet width controlled by bearing

Depth by height of cutter in relation to work

DIAGRAM 4

PRACTICAL "UTILITY" BIT

Straight

DIAGRAM 5

MULTIPURPOSE BIT
Dozens of shapes are possible by using part of the profile or by making multiple cuts

DIAGRAM 6

CARBIDE-TIPPED "STARTER" SETS

BASIC FUNCTION

1–1/4" straight
2–3/4" straight
3–mortising
4–*round nose
5–V-groove
6–dovetail
7–*cove
8–*rabbeting
9–*roundover
10–*ogee
11–*chamfer
12–flush trim

#1 & 2   #3   #4

#5   #6   #7

#8   #9   #10

#11   #12

NOTE-All 12 bits are included in starter set (about $167). Bits marked with an * included in a 6 piece set (about $109).

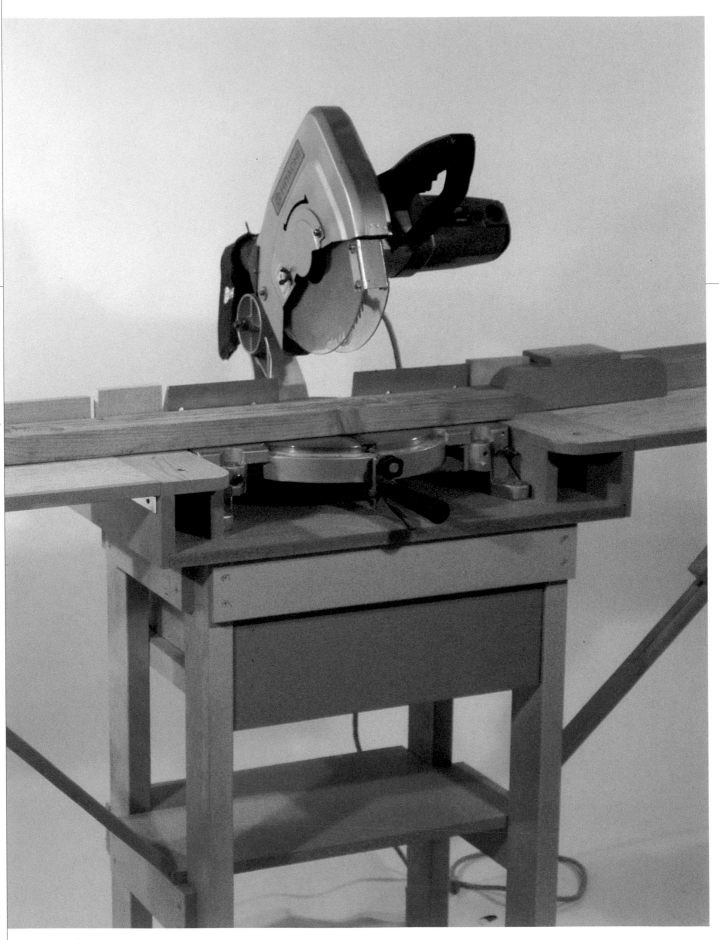

Miter Saw Workstation

**This is a must-have accessory for your chop saw,
and it tucks nicely into almost any corner.**

Miter saws are fine tools, but even the best of them — those that are equipped with extensions — don't provide adequate support surface for the jobs they are designed for. My favorite lumberyard has a chop saw set up on a sturdy stand with fixed wings so it can easily and safely support a 12' (or longer) 2×4. That's a fine setup for a barn-size workshop, but when I thought about a similar setup for myself, I had to consider space limitations.

It didn't take a brainstorm to envision a special stand for my miter saw that had hinged extension tables that would fold down when the saw wasn't in use. And there were some other features that came to mind, such as a stop that's usable on either side of the saw, a storage drawer and an accessory that makes it easier to produce accurate compound miter cuts.

The size of the unit is suitable for most any saw (all that I've examined anyway), but you might want to check the width of your machine and, if necessary, change the width of the stand's top. It should be wide enough to accommodate the saw plus the two short extensions that are permanently attached to it.

MAKE THE BASIC BASE
Begin by cutting the legs, the three longer rails and the four side rails to length. Cut a ¾"-deep by 1½"-wide rabbet at each end of the rails. You can make the rabbets with a dado stack, but results will be better if you use a tenoning jig. Saw the shoulder cuts first, working in normal crosscut position, then use the jig to make the cheek cuts.

ASSEMBLE THE BASE
Start the assembly by applying glue to the rabbet cuts in the side rails and holding them in place against the legs with clamps. Then drill holes for and install the No. 10 × 1½" fh screws. Before going further, attach the drawer rails (D) to the insides of the legs with glue and 6d finishing nails.

Next add the two rear rails and the front one, again after coating the rabbets with glue. While the assembly is "open," install the two top drawer rails. Glue alone is enough here if you keep the parts in place with clamps, but you can toenail through the top of the guides into the legs if you wish. The purpose of the top rails is to keep the drawer from tilting when you pull it out.

The final step for the substructure is to cut the shelf to overall size and then notch it at the back two corners so it will fit the rear legs. Attach the shelf with glue and 6d nails.

The top for the stand has a ⅜"-deep

by ¾"-wide groove running across its length. The forward shoulder of the groove must align with the bearing surface of the tool's fences. So place the tool on the stand and check for correct position before you form the groove. Attach the top with No. 10 × 1½" fh screws and then, with the tool centered, drill the holes that are needed to bolt the tool in place.

EXTENSION TABLES
The materials list offers dimensions for the components that make up the short extensions, but they should be checked against the tool's position and the height of its table. Start by preparing the end piece, making sure that its height above the top of the stand equals that of the tool's table less ¾".

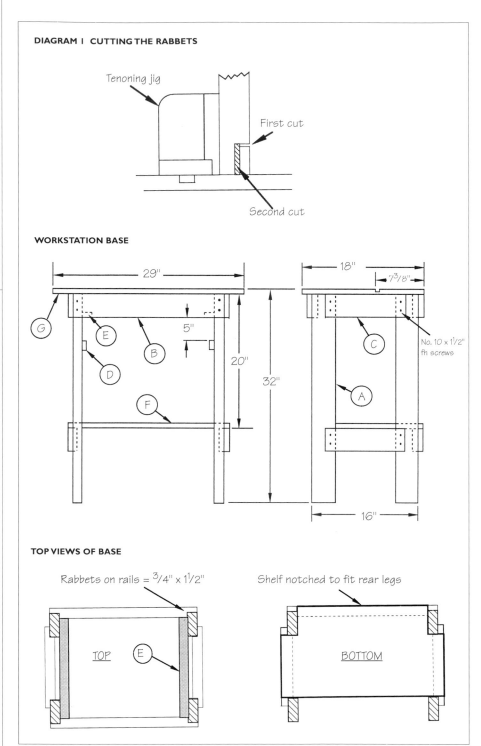

DIAGRAM I CUTTING THE RABBETS

Tenoning jig

First cut

Second cut

WORKSTATION BASE

29"

G

E

B

D

F

5"

20"

32"

18"

7³/₈"

C

No. 10 x 1¹/₂"
fh screws

A

16"

TOP VIEWS OF BASE

Rabbets on rails = ³/₄" x 1¹/₂"

Shelf notched to fit rear legs

TOP   E

BOTTOM

THE JIGS & FIXTURES BIBLE

Schedule of Materials: MITER SAW STAND

No.	Part	Item	Dimensions T W L	Material
4	A	Legs	1¹/₂" x 3¹/₂" x 31¹/₄"	Fir
3	B	Rails	1¹/₂" x 3¹/₂" x 22¹/₂"	Fir
4	C	Side rails	1¹/₂" x 3¹/₂" x 12"	Fir
2	D	Drawer rails	³/₄" x 1¹/₂" x 15¹/₄"	Fir
2	E	Drawer rails	³/₄" x 1¹/₂" x 14¹/₂"	Fir
1	F	Shelf	³/₄" x 13¹/₄" x 24"	Plywood
1	G	Top	³/₄" x 18" x 29"	Plywood

Form the rabbet at the bottom edge of the end piece and then the dado that should mate with the groove that is in the stand's top. Attach the component with glue and 4d nails.

Using glue and 4d nails, attach the fence, which fits in the groove that is the stand's top and in the dado in the end piece. Cut the support short enough so it won't interfere with a full swing of the tool's indexing handle. Put the support in place with glue and 4d nails and then add the glue blocks to strengthen the assembly. The last step is to add the table with glue and 6d finishing nails. When forming the components for the short extensions, remember that the assemblies are left and right.

DROP-DOWN EXTENSIONS

When you begin assembling the drop-down extensions, remember that like the short extensions, there are left and right wings. Cut the two tables to size and then add the trim strips with glue and 6d finishing nails. Form the ³/₈"-deep by ³/₄"-wide rabbet along the bottom edge of the fence and add it to the table with glue and 5d box nails. Be sure the angle between fence and table is 90°.

INSTALL THE HINGES

Follow this procedure to make sure the fences of the project will be accurately aligned. First remove the tool from the stand. Turn the stand over and place it on the workbench so the fence of the short extensions butts against the edge of the workbench. Place the drop-down extension so its fence also butts against the workbench edge, and use a clamp to keep the component in position.

Install the piano hinge and then add the backflap hinge. The project can remain in this position while you prepare the braces. Make the top one first and, after installing the ³/₈" threaded insert, attach it to the backflap hinge. The bottom brace is slotted at one end and notched at the other end so it can rest solidly against the stand's shelf. The slot is needed for table-level

DIAGRAM 2 SHORT FENCE/TABLE EXTENSIONS

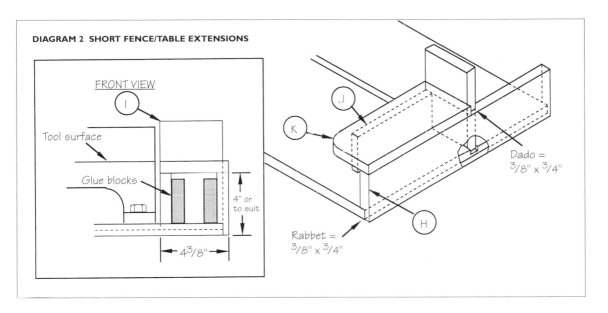

FRONT VIEW

I

Tool surface

Glue blocks

4" or to suit

4³/8"

J

K

H

Dado = ³/8" x ³/4"

Rabbet = ³/8" x ³/4"

Schedule of Materials: **SHORT EXTENSIONS**

No.	Part	Item	Dimensions T W L	Material
2	H	End pieces	³/4" x 4" x 18"	Pine
2	I	Fences	³/4" x 4" x 7"	Pine
2	J	Supports	³/4" x 3¹/4" x 8¹/2"	Pine
2	K	Tables	³/4" x 4³/8" x 10⁵/8"	Pine

DIAGRAM 3 BRACE DETAIL

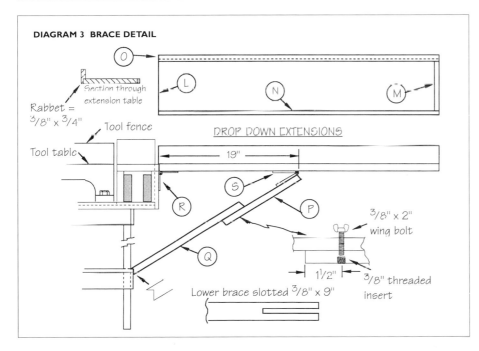

O

L

N

M

Section through extension table

Rabbet = ³/8" x ³/4"

Tool fence

Tool table

DROP DOWN EXTENSIONS

19"

S

R

P

Q

³/8" x 2" wing bolt

1¹/2"

³/8" threaded insert

Lower brace slotted ³/8" x 9"

Schedule of Materials: **FOLDING EXTENSIONS**

No.	Part	Item	Dimensions T W L	Material
2	L	Tables	³/4" x 10¹/2" x 29"	Plywood
2	M	Trim pieces	¹/2" x ³/4" x 10¹/2"	Fir
2	N	Trim	¹/2" x ³/4" x 29"	Fir
2	O	Fences	³/4" x 3³/4" x 29"	Fir
2	P	Top braces	1" x 1¹/2" x 14"	Fir
2	Q	Bot. braces	1" x 1¹/2" x 20"	Fir
2	R	Piano hinges	1¹/2" x 10¹/2"	
2	S	Flap hinges	1¹/2" x 1¹/2" x 2"	

adjustment and so the braces can be "folded" out of the way when the extensions are lowered. Details for the braces are shown in diagram 3.

SAW STOP

The stop is designed so it will function on either extension table and it can be inverted when necessary. Cut all the parts to size but adjust the width of the top so the gap between the front and back will be ³/4" plus about ¹/32". Install the ³/8" threaded insert in the back component and then assemble the pieces with glue and No. 10 × 1¹/4" fh screws.

DRAWER

The drawer design isn't fancy but the unit is sturdy and suits the purpose. Start with the bottom, making sure that it slides smoothly between the legs of the stand. Cut the front to size and form the groove for the bottom and the dadoes for the sides. Prepare the sides and then assemble the four pieces with glue and finishing nails. The guides are installed in line with the sides, but before attaching them permanently, check to see that they will slide smoothly along the drawer rails in the stand. Finally, use glue and 6d finishing nails to install the back. You don't need a handle because the lip below the bottom of the drawer serves nicely.

DIAGRAM 4 ATTACHING THE EXTENSIONS

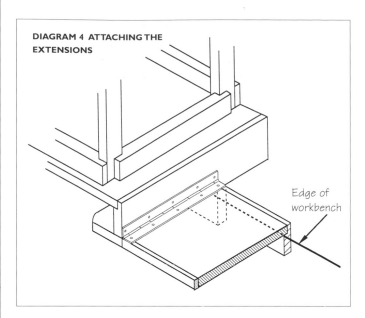

Edge of workbench

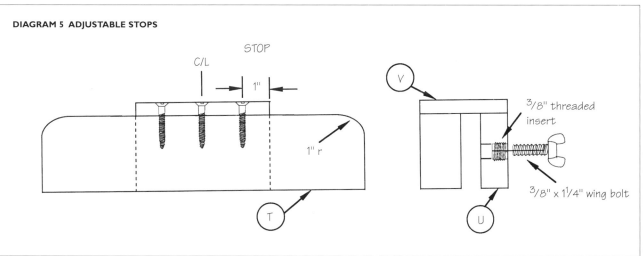

Schedule of Materials: STOP

No.	Part	Item	Dimensions T W L	Material
1	T	Front	$1\frac{1}{2}$" x $2\frac{3}{4}$" x 12"	Fir
1	U	Back	1" x $2\frac{3}{4}$" x 5"	Fir
1	V	Top	$\frac{1}{2}$" x $3\frac{17}{32}$" x 5"	Fir

Schedule of Materials: DRAWER

No.	Part	Item	Dimensions T W L	Material
1	W	Bottom	$\frac{1}{4}$" x 15" x $19\frac{1}{2}$"	Plywood
1	X	Front	$\frac{1}{4}$" x $6\frac{1}{2}$" x $19\frac{1}{2}$"	Plywood
2	Y	Sides	$\frac{1}{4}$" x $4\frac{1}{4}$" x 15"	Plywood
2	Z	Guides	$\frac{1}{4}$" x $1\frac{1}{4}$" x 15"	Fir
1	AA	Back	$\frac{1}{4}$" x $4\frac{1}{4}$" x $16\frac{1}{2}$"	Plywood

DIAGRAM 5 ADJUSTABLE STOPS

STOP

C/L

1"

1" r

$\frac{3}{8}$" threaded insert

$\frac{3}{8}$" x $1\frac{1}{4}$" wing bolt

T

V

U

DIAGRAM 6 DRAWER

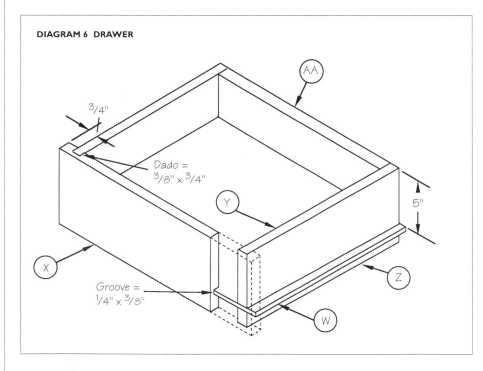

AA

$\frac{3}{4}$"

Dado = $\frac{3}{8}$" x $\frac{3}{4}$"

Y

5"

X

Groove = $\frac{1}{4}$" x $\frac{3}{8}$"

W

Z

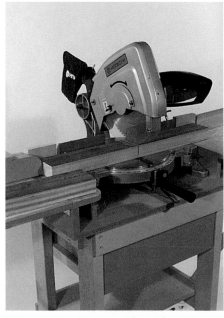

The stop functions on either side of the saw can be inverted if necessary.

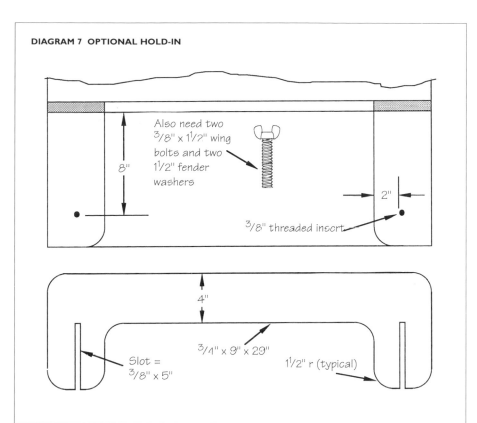

DIAGRAM 7 OPTIONAL HOLD-IN

8"

Also need two
3/8" x 11/2" wing
bolts and two
11/2" fender
washers

2"

3/8" threaded insert

4"

Slot =
3/8" x 5"

3/4" x 9" x 29"

11/2" r (typical)

HOLDING JIG

This hold-in isn't essential for the table's normal functions, but you'll find it handy when making compound cuts. The hold-in acts as a brace so your work can be held at a sloping angle against the fence. For example, if the saw is set for a 45° miter, the result will be a compound cut regardless of the work's slope angle. Even if your saw can be tilted for bevel cuts, the hold-in is desirable because it eliminates one of the critical compound angle settings.

Anyway, the accessory calls for installing two ⅜" threaded inserts in the tables of the short extensions, locating them as shown in the drawing. Cut the hold-in to overall shape and form the slots before producing the final shape.

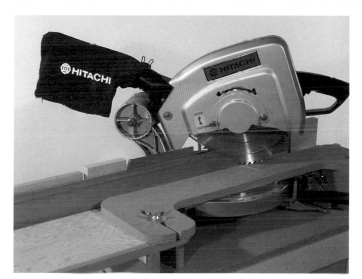

Using the hold-in eliminates the need for one of the critical compound angle settings — the blade tilt angle. Cove moulding establishes its own slope angle.

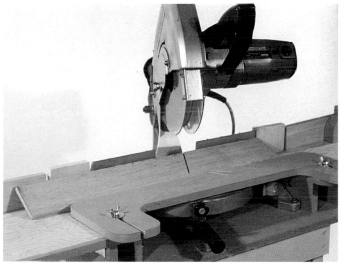

The slope angle on flat stock can be established with a bevel, or set arbitrarily. For example, when making a picture frame with sloping sides, it won't matter too much if the slope is off a few degrees so long as it's visually pleasing.

Master Table Saw Jig

Make a Swiss Army jig for your table saw.

The Master Jig remains one of the most popular shop-made accessories for a table saw. It's a do-anything project that has add-on "modules" that enhance convenience, accuracy, production output and safety — on both routine and not-so-routine cuts.

Popular Woodworking last presented the master jig in the January 1994 issue. And since that time, the jig (which is on my saw more than it is off) has been modified to the point where it seemed wise to rebuild it from scratch.

The "new" jig has the practical aspects of the original, with several improvements, including

- Easier-to-produce table inserts for use with a saw blade or dado tool.
- A more professional fence with a built-in adjustable stop.
- A redesigned, more flexible tenoning attachment that includes a swiveling guide so, for example, forming spline grooves in miter cuts is not limited to those of 45°.
- A tapering jig.
- Thoughts on how to add notching jigs for producing odd-shaped components or making cuts that might not be safe using conventional means.

The principle advantage of the project is that it is essentially a sliding

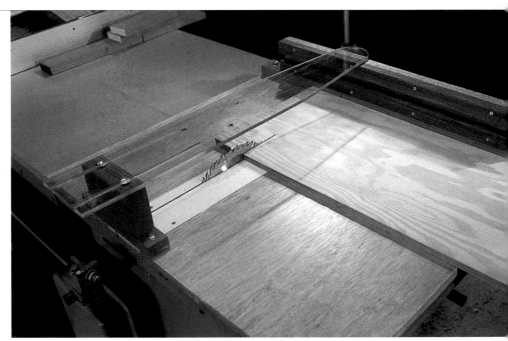

The basic master jig, shown here, has six modules you can attach to perform different operations.

table. All the components are secured to the main table so that regardless of the operation — crosscutting, mitering, dadoing, tapering, forming tenons or grooves in miters for splines or feathers — the work and the jig move together. This eliminates the friction normally present when work contacts the saw's table directly, and it minimizes the amount of hand pressure you must apply to the work to secure it while sawing.

When making miter cuts, special guides on the master jig eliminate "creep" — the accuracy-spoiling bugaboo that is always present when doing

such work with just the miter gauge. When doing tenoning operations with either a saw blade or a dadoing tool, the work is held securely in the jig's tenoning accessory. This improves accuracy and is much safer than handholding narrow stock on edge while moving it along the rip fence. Even simple crosscutting is easier and more accurate because the jig's fence gives more support surface than the face of a miter gauge.

Overall, the master jig is a collection of essential but usually separate jigs that has the advantages of a sliding table for each of them.

CONSTRUCTION PROCEDURES

The master jig in my shop is sized for a 10" Delta Unisaw, which has a 27" × 28¼" table. Many 9" and 10" machines (the most popular sizes) are similar, so the dimensions in the drawings may be applicable without drastic changes. Check for necessary conversions before cutting material.

The jig's table thickness reduces the maximum projection of the saw blade, but because a 10" blade will project 3" or more from the table, the reduction is not critical. An 8" or 9" blade can be used with the jig for many woodworking jobs. For dadoing, it's necessary to use an 8" unit to allow the blades to extend above the slot.

Accurate construction is important, although some tolerances are built in. For example, the fastening holes in the attachments are ⅜" in diameter, even though they are secured with 5/16" bolts that thread into the threaded inserts installed in the table. This allows for minor alignment adjustments when putting the attachments in place. If necessary, because of human error, the ⅜" holes can be enlarged an additional 1/16".

IN GENERAL

Careful attention to construction details is essential for this jig to perform efficiently; it's a lifetime shop accessory and will be on your table saw, as mine is, more times than not. Previewing each construction step before performing it makes sense. Sand components before and after assembly. Apply two (or more) coats of sanding sealer to all surfaces and edges, sanding between coats and after the final one. Occasional applications of paste wax rubbed to a polish on the saw's table and the underside of the sliding table are a good idea.

1. The Table Itself

Cut the table and the top left and right parts to size and join them with contact cement. I decided on this assembly because it makes it easy to put in the removable inserts. The original one-piece table required some precise router work for installation of the inserts.

Carefully lay out the location of all the threaded inserts that must be installed in the table. Spot their locations with a center punch and drill 1/16" pilot holes. Enlarge the holes to ½" diameter drilling from the top surface and using a backup block on the underside. The holes are close enough to the edges of the table so the drilling can be done on a drill press to ensure squareness. Install the threaded inserts through the bottom of the table until they are almost flush with the table's top surface.

Shape the hardwood guide bars on the bottom of the jig to suit the miter-gauge slots in your saw. The bars should slide smoothly in the slots without wobble. Place the bars in position on the saw's top and then place the jig's table on top so its left side and front edge are aligned with the same edges on the table saw's top. Use slim brads at each end and at a center point to tack-nail through the jig's table to keep the bars in correct position. Drill clearance and pilot holes, and countersink for the screws. If you don't do this, the screws might spread the bars so they will fit too tightly in the table slots. Then attach the bars permanently with three No. 6 × ⅞" flathead (fh) screws through the underside of each bar.

Next, cut the inserts to the size indicated in the Schedule of Materials and mark the location of the attachment screws on one of them. Clamp the inserts together as a pad, and, with the marked one serving as a template, drill through them for the six No. 6 × ⅝" fh screws. Install one insert, countersinking carefully, so the screws will be flush with the table's surface. Now you can form the initial saw-kerf.

Use a good saw blade, preferably a high-quality carbide-tipped combination blade that will always be used with the jig. With the machine shut down, lower the blade so it is below the table's surface and then use a clamp or two to secure the sliding table in correct position. Turn on the machine and slowly raise the blade until it cuts through the insert. Remove the clamps and advance the table to extend the kerf length to about 12". An exact kerf length is not critical at this point.

Repeat the procedure with a second insert to form a dado slot through both the sliding table and the insert. (You can do this later when you need to work with a dadoing tool.)

TABLE PLAN VIEW

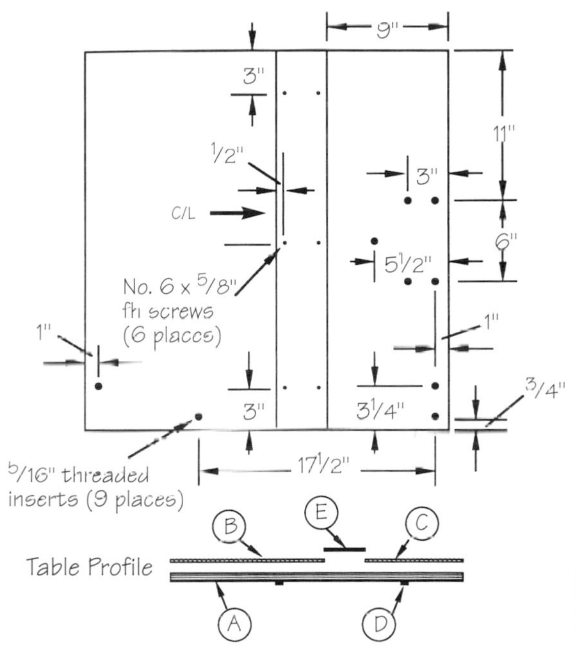

Schedule of Materials: **MASTER JIG TABLE**

No.	Part	Item	Dimensions T W L	Material
A	1	Table	½" x 27" x 28¼"	Plywood
B	1	Top left	¼" x 15½" x 27"	Plywood
C	1	Top right	¼" x 9" x 27"	Plywood
D	2	Guide bars	⅜" x ¾" x 27"	Hardwood
E	2	Inserts	¼" x 3¾" x 27"	Plywood

2. Assemble the Fence

First cut the back (F) to exact size and then install the ¼" threaded insert for the thumbscrew that locks the stop slide bar (H). Locate the threaded insert so it is about 3" to the left of the kerf in the table.

The rabbet cuts in the retainers (G) and the slide bar can be formed by using a dado or by making two passes with a saw blade.

Attach the top retainer to the back with four No. 6 × 1¼" fh screws and then, using the slide bar for positioning, add the bottom retainer in the same way. If necessary, sand the slide bar so it will move easily. Cut the base (I) to size, and after drilling the ⅜" holes at each end, add it to the fence by gluing and clamping.

The final step is to attach the stop (J), which is a steel or aluminum angle, to the end of the slide bar. Use thin washers between the angle and the bar so the stop won't rub against the retainer.

FENCE ASSEMBLY

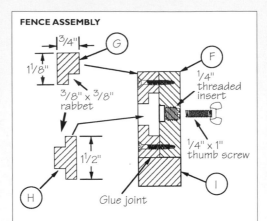

Glue joint

ATTACH THE STOP

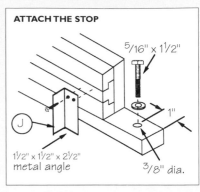

Schedule of Materials: **MASTER JIG FENCE**

No.	Part	Item	Dimensions T W L	Material
1	F	Back	¾" × 3" × 23¼"	Hardwood
2	G	Retainers	¾" × 1⅛" × 23¼"	Hardwood
1	H	Slide bar	¾" × 1½" × 23¼"	Hardwood
1	I	Base	1" × 1½" × 28¼"	Hardwood
1	J	Stop	1½" × 1½" × 2½"	Metal

3. Miter Guides

The triangular guide (K) is used when miter cuts are made consecutively on a piece of stock that is long enough to supply the parts you need. Use the V-shaped guide (L) when the frame components have been precut to length. Mark the 45° angles on each guide with a combination square or a draftsman's template. It's a good idea to saw almost to the lines and then finish by sanding. In each case, for the sake of accuracy, bolt the stock in place on the sliding table and use a straightedge placed flush against the side of the saw blade to mark a center line for the angles.

The hold-downs (M) are simple, but they work when secured to the guides with screws (see photo). A good way to form the slot for the screw is to drill a ³⁄₁₆" hole where the slot ends and then clean out the waste with a scroll saw, band saw or even a handsaw.

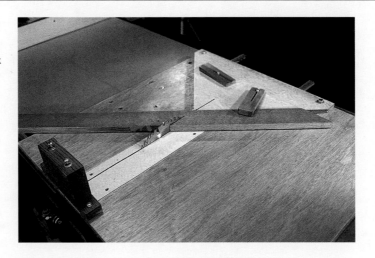

Schedule of Materials: **MASTER JIG MITER GUIDES**

No.	Part	Item	Dimensions T W L	Material
1	K	Tri-guide	½" × 11½" × 20"	Plywood
1	L	V-guide	½" × 11½" × 20"	Plywood
2	M	Hold-downs	⅝" × 1½" × 5¼"	Hardwood

TRIANGULAR GUIDE

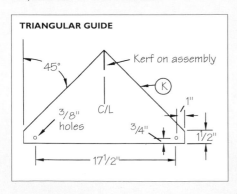

HOLD-DOWNS

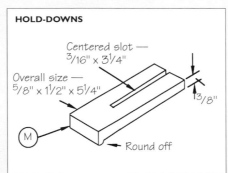

V-SHAPED GUIDE

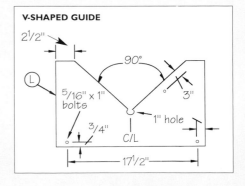

4. The Tenoning Jig

Cut the face (N) of the accessory to size and then carefully lay out the locations of all the holes. The top line of holes (either $5/16$" or $1/4$") are through holes that are needed for the swivel guide. The remaining four holes are bored for the $3/16$" threaded inserts that are used when working with the tenoning jig's miter guides.

After all the holes are drilled and the threaded inserts are installed, rabbet the bottom edge of the face $3/8$" deep by $3/4$" wide to accept the $3/4$" base.

Cut the base (O) to size and then lay out the center lines for the slots that must be formed. Bore end holes and then clean away the waste by making saw cuts. The center $5/16$" slot allows the jig to be moved in relation to the saw blade. A $5/16$" x $1 1/4$" bolt secures the setting.

To make the sides (P), start with a piece that is more than 14" long and then, after forming the $3/8$"-deep by $3/4$"-wide rabbet along one edge, saw the part to get two pieces. It's good to remember that these are left- and right-hand parts when you round off one of the top corners.

Next try a dry assembly of the three components (base, sides and face) to be sure the angle between the face and the base is 90°. When you're certain of the alignment, assemble the parts with glue and No. 10 x $1 1/2$" fh screws.

The guide bars for the tenoning jig (Q) are straightforward, but be sure their widths are exactly 1".

The swivel guide is used as a vertical guide when making cheek cuts for a tenon. Use a square to be sure the angle between the bearing edge of the guide and the table is 90° before securing the guide. Use a $5/16$" carriage bolt through the guide's pivot hole and a $1/4$" carriage bolt through the groove.

Schedule of Materials: **MASTER JIG TENONING JIG**

No.	Part	Item	Dimensions T W L	Material
1	N	Face	$3/4$" x 8" x $16 1/2$"	Hardwood
1	O	Base	$3/4$" x $7 3/4$" x 14"	Hardwood
2	P	Sides	$3/4$" x $5 1/4$" x 7"	Hardwood
2	Q	Guide bars	$3/4$" x 1" x 5"	Hardwood

TENONING JIG FACE VIEW

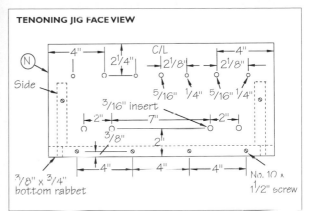

BASE

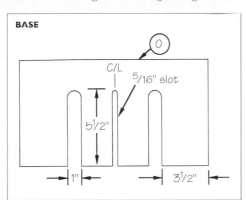

SIDES

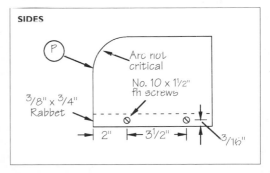

GUIDE BARS

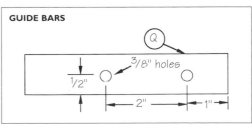

5. Tenoning Jig Attachments

The miter guides (R) used with the tenoning jig are triangular pieces with 8" sides. Although they are secured to the jig's face with $^3/_{16}$" screws, the attachment holes are $^1/_4$". This allows some room for adjustment when the guides are set up (photo at right).

Cut the swivel guide (S) to size and then form the $^1/_4$" semicircular groove (see photo, lower right). You can do this by drilling end holes and removing the waste on a scroll saw or even with a coping saw. But, if possible, a compass arm jig forms the groove easily with a router. If you work this way, make repeat passes, projecting the bit an extra $^1/_8$" or so for each one.

Both guides are used when forming grooves for feathers that will be used to reinforce the miter joint. Always place the same surface of each part against the face of the jig. Thus the grooves will mesh, even though they might not be exactly centered.

TENONING JIG MITER GUIDES

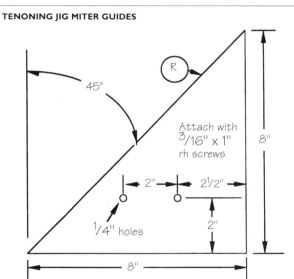

45°

R

Attach with $^3/_{16}$" x 1" rh screws

8"

2"

2$^1/_2$"

2"

$^1/_4$" holes

8"

TENONING JIG SWIVEL GUIDE

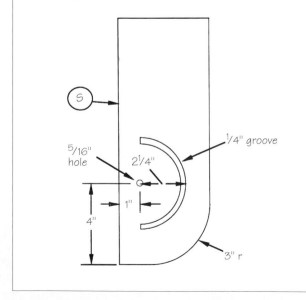

S

$^1/_4$" groove

$^5/_{16}$" hole

2$^1/_4$"

1"

4"

3" r

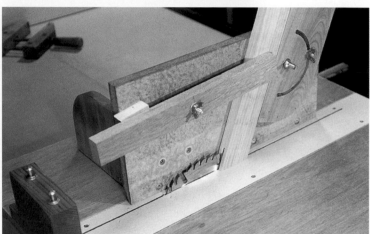

The advantage of the swivel guide is that it can be set to accommodate angles other than 45°. It can be positioned using any of the top holes in the jig, and it also can be inverted. Note that a scrap piece of wood is used under the free end of the hold-down.

HOLD-DOWN

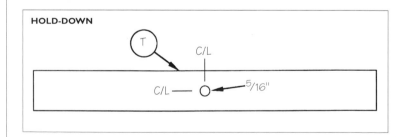

T

C/L

C/L

$^5/_{16}$"

Schedule of Materials: MASTER JIG TENONING JIG ATTACHMENTS

No.	Part	Item	Dimensions T W L	Material
2	R	Miter guides	$^1/_4$" x 8" x 8"	Plywood
1	S	Swivel guide	$^3/_4$" x 4$^1/_4$" x 12"	Hardwood
2	T	Hold-down	$^3/_4$" x 1$^1/_2$" x 13"	Hardwood

6. Don't Forget the Guard

I used Lexan for the guard but any clear, rigid plastic will do. The guard spans across the table for crosscutting and dadoing, but the slots allow other positions that are more suitable when, for example, using the table's miter guides. Form the slots, as I have suggested for others, by drilling end holes and then sawing away the waste.

Install the support so it and the kerf in the table will have a common center line.

GUARD AND SUPPORT

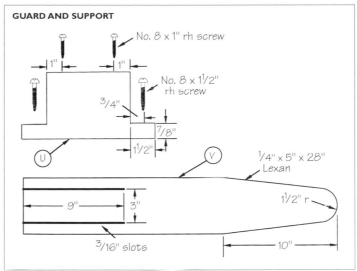

Though I removed the guard for many of these photos for clarity, it's essential part of the Master Jig.

Schedule of Materials: **MASTER JIG GUARD**

No.	Part	Item	Dimensions T W L	Material
1	U	Support	1½" x 4" x 8"	Hardwood
1	V	Guard	¼" x 5" x 28"	Lexan

7. A Few Extras

Notching jigs must be custom designed for particular applications. The cutout in the jig can fit the part that is needed or the section that must be removed from the component.

The taper jig, as designed, is pretty flexible and is useful for many taper-cutting chores. Actually, it's feasible to make special ones when you need to produce many parts of similar shape.

Notching jigs and the taper jig are locked in place using the same threaded insert that's installed to secure the tenoning jig.

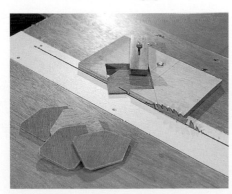

Here is shown a typical notching jig in use. Note that the hold-down for the table's miter jigs comes in handy for this application. Secure the hold-down with a rh woodscrew.

SAMPLE NOTCHING JIG   **TAPER JIG**

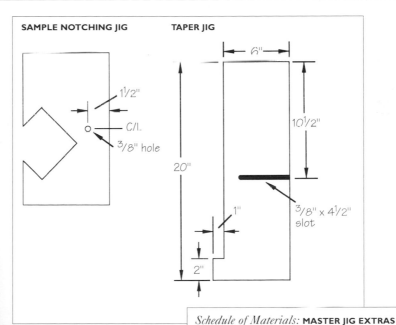

Schedule of Materials: **MASTER JIG EXTRAS**

No.	Item	Dimensions T W L	Material
1	Taper jig	½" x 7" x 20"	Plywood
1	Notching jig	½" x 6" x 10½"	Plywood

Special jigs can be made for particular taper-cutting chores. Note the hold-down that keeps hands away from the cutting area.

Maintain Your Handsaws Like a Pro

Get rid of those ragged cuts for good with these saw tune-up tips.

A dull handsaw is irritating, and it can be painful to both your projects and you. Rough cuts, ragged edges and tired arms contribute nothing to top-quality woodworking and lessen enjoyment. In truth, we have a simple choice to make: Keep equipment in top condition or suffer unnecessary frustration and poor results.

Maintaining handsaws in mint condition doesn't require membership in a secret society. A few special tools are needed and, as there are more than a few teeth on a saw, some patience is necessary.

You may ask why you should sharpen your own handsaws since professional sharpening services are available. I know of two reasons: It isn't easy to find a sharpener who's devoted to the craft, and when I'm involved with a project and realize my sawing tool needs attention, I don't want the tool and the project put on hold. I want the saw rejuvenated now!

WHAT IS A SAW?

Knowing a saw blade's characteristics is a good first step. Common handsaws are designed for ripping (cutting lengthwise with the grain) or crosscutting (working across the grain or at an angle to it). Finesse tools like backsaws and dovetail saws are essentially crosscut saws. How the tools perform their

functions depends on the design of the teeth, and that's a critical factor in the sharpening process.

Whether a saw cuts "coarse" or "fine" relates to the number of points per inch (ppi). To know the number of teeth per inch, just deduct one from the ppi. The more ppi, the smaller the teeth, which leads to slower but smoother results. That's why backsaws and dovetail saws have a lot more ppi than common ripsaws or crosscut saws.

Saw teeth are shaped for the job they must do (see diagram). Teeth for crosscutting are designed to move

across the grain like so many small, sharp knives. The teeth are bevel filed and the cutting edges slant at a sharp angle so a shearing action, as opposed to a chiseling action, results. Rip teeth are filed straight across and have cutting edges that are almost perpendicular to the blade. This is efficient for cutting with the grain. Each tooth performs like a tiny chisel, chipping out its own bit of wood. If you examine the waste from sawing operations, you'll see that crosscut saws produce sawdust, while a ripsaw spews out small chips of wood.

SHARPENING PHASES

Sharpening handsaws involves jointing, setting, filing and, optionally, side jointing.

Jointing, which is accomplished by passing a mill file across the tops of the teeth in a heel-to-toe direction, is done to verify that all teeth have the same height. Jointing can be done freehand, but that's risky. It's wise to acquire a commercial jointer or make one along the designs detailed in diagram 1. The idea is to make as few light passes as needed — only until you can see a bright spot on the tip of each tooth. The amount of jointing must be judged by the saw's condition. If the tool is fairly new and has been cared for, jointing may not even be necessary. I don't believe it's necessary every time you sharpen the saw.

Setting means bending the upper one-third to one-half the length of each tooth with alternate teeth pointing in an opposite direction. It's done so the kerf will be wider than the gauge, or thickness, of the blade. This is necessary so the blade moves through its kerf without binding.

To do this operation freehand is out of the question. This is where a saw set, which costs about $17, comes in to use. The tool, which operates with pliers-like handles, performs two operations simultaneously: A block presses and holds the saw blade on an anvil, and a beveled punch, or plunger, bends the tooth onto the inclined section of the anvil (diagram 2). The anvil on the tool I use is an adjustable wheel with numbered settings that closely correspond to the ppi of a saw. Set the number to an index mark and the anvil is positioned so all teeth will be bent an equal amount. I can't guarantee that all saw sets work the same way, so it's important to read the instructions provided with the tool.

RIPSAW

52°

8°

CROSSCUT SAW

15° 45°

Here are common tooth angles for ripsaws and crosscut saws.

This shows how files are positioned for the sharpening stage.

kerf width

kerf width

Note the difference between teeth on ripsaws and crosscut saws.

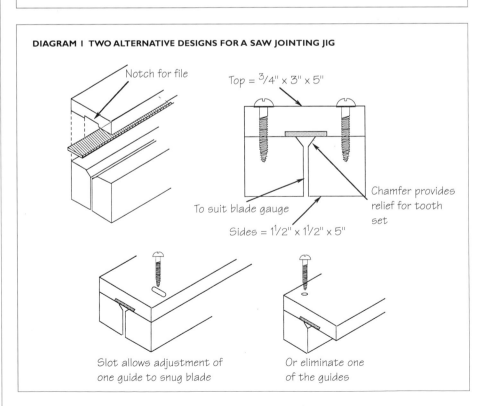

DIAGRAM I TWO ALTERNATIVE DESIGNS FOR A SAW JOINTING JIG

Notch for file

Top = ³/4" x 3" x 5"

To suit blade gauge

Chamfer provides relief for tooth set

Sides = 1¹/2" x 1¹/2" x 5"

Slot allows adjustment of one guide to snug blade

Or eliminate one of the guides

Anyway, with the saw clamped in a vise or between boards, start at the heel end and set each tooth that points away from you. Then reverse the saw and repeat the operation on the alternate teeth. Be sure to check whether you may have missed a tooth or two. The set must be uniform throughout if the saw is to cut straight.

Filing, which actually sharpens the teeth, can be viewed two ways. One is as a touch-up chore (like occasionally stropping a razor) when the saw is in respectable condition to begin with. It also can be seen as renovation, when it's just a step in a complete sharpening cycle. In either case, clamp the saw between boards in a vise so the teeth project a bit above the top of the boards. The idea is to prevent the blade from chattering and to minimize the screeching noise caused by filing.

Now place the correct size of tapered file (see chart) in the gullet that's on the left of the first tooth that's set toward you. For a crosscut saw, place the file across the blade, then swing it left to 60°. Keep the file horizontal and snug in the gullet. File on the forward stroke only, lifting the file to reset it for another stroke. Stroke only as many times as needed to remove half the flat made when

file selection chart

PPI*	FILE TO USE
4½, 5½, 6	7" slim taper
7, 8	6" slim taper
9, 10	6" slim taper
11, 12, 13, 14, 15	4½" slim taper
More than 16	5" superfine (No. 2 cut)

points per inch

jointing. Repeat the procedure in alternate gullets for the length of the saw. Then reverse the saw and repeat the operation.

Ripsaws are treated in similar fashion except that filing is done straight across (at a right angle to the blade).

Needless to say, success in this venture depends primarily on your degree of expertise with a file. If you're just touching up, the file's position can be determined by the existing angles of the teeth — just position the file accordingly. If you're doing a complete job, then application of the file becomes more critical.

If at this point you're exclaiming, "Oh golly!" don't despair. There's another option, namely, a saw sharpening jig of the type shown set up in the photo. This jig is adjustable so correct angles and planes are established for various saw blades, including circular ones. All you must do is concentrate on stroking the file that's included.

Side jointing is a last, optional step done with the fine side of an oilstone as shown in diagram 3. The operation dresses the points of the teeth to exact alignment. The idea is to prepare the saw to make the smoothest cuts possible. Apply pressure with just the weight of the stone; a couple of strokes on each side of the blade are enough to do the job.

Like all tools with edges for cutting, proper sharpening not only gives the best results with the least effort but also gives the user greater satisfaction from the work at hand.

DIAGRAM 2 SAW SET TOOL

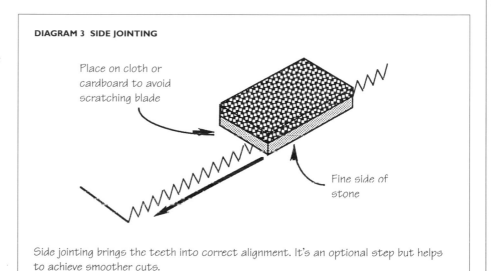

Anvil — beveled at top edge

Anvil

Plunger

The saw set has a plunger or ram that bends teeth against a beveled anvil. The tool has handles like a pair of pliers.

DIAGRAM 3 SIDE JOINTING

Place on cloth or cardboard to avoid scratching blade

Fine side of stone

Side jointing brings the teeth into correct alignment. It's an optional step but helps to achieve smoother cuts.

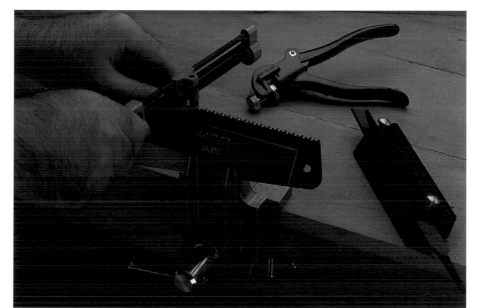

The saw sharpening jig is adjustable to suit the saw being worked on. It assures that all teeth will be filed to correct angles. Your only concern will be stroking the file.

The Moulding Cutterhead

Are you overlooking a practical accessory

for your table saw?

Moulding heads, often called moulding cutterheads or shaper heads, were available before carbide-tipped saw blades became common and, in fact, before portable routers became "in" tools. The term *moulding* isn't the whole story. While the accessory, with an assortment of knives, is efficient for production of standard or original moulding designs, it is also a practical tool for producing various classic joints, applying decorative details like flutes or beads to furniture components, and for other applications such as shaping the edges of slabs and forming cabinet door lips. While I have my share of portable routers, I often rely on the moulding head for those times when it's more convenient to bring the work to the tool.

THE MOULDING HEAD

Moulding heads may be comparatively heavy or light and can differ in configuration, but each type has three slots equally spaced around the perimeter to accommodate a matched set of knives. Some units are supplied with a bushing and/or spacer so that they can be correctly mounted on the saw's arbor. Be attentive to the moulding-head information in the machine's owner's manual and to the instructions that come with the accessory. An important factor is the length of the saw's arbor. This

may dictate how thick the head can be. In any event, there must be sufficient threaded area, after the head is mounted, for the arbor nut to seat.

Some table saws, especially small ones, can't handle moulding heads, or must be used with knives of a particular size and shape. In general, moulding heads are interchangeable between various brands of table saws, but check with your manufacturer first.

TABLE INSERT

Like a dadoing tool, a moulding head makes wider cuts than a saw blade, so it must be used with an insert that has a wide opening for the knives. This insert is a special unit: The one you may have on hand for dado work won't do.

The standard insert for moulding chores will do for general use, but there will be times when it's good practice to furnish one that allows customizing the opening for minimum clearance around the knives. You can make your own by using the regular insert as a pattern or purchase ready-made blank ones from mail-order houses. Either way, be sure the new insert fits tightly in the table. Form the opening by setting the blank insert in place after lowering the head so the knives are below the table's surface. Set the rip fence so it serves as a hold-down (using shims if necessary) and then slowly raise the head until the knives project to the depth of cut needed.

MOULDING KNIVES

There are three classes of moulding knives. Combination types are designed so that a portion of the profile may be used to produce a particular form. For example, one part of the knife makes a bead, the other cuts a quarter-round profile. Single-purpose units are meant for full-profile cuts. Sets of knives will produce complementary shapes. The basic function of a profile may be specific, but there is no rule that you limit any knife to a particular chore. You can opt to use any portion of any profile if the result suits your design. After some experience you will find that partial cuts from two or more knives can result in a form that can't be achieved with a single knife.

Many knife shapes are available. Those shown here are typical but are not a complete library. Some catalogs offer as many as 40 profiles. The options are nice and won't be confusing if you start by selecting knives that suit your current work interests — decorative edges, cope cuts for frames, reed or flute details, forming joints. Both Delta and Sears, for example, offer sets that include the moulding head and three or four knife sets of popular profiles. That's a wise, economical beginning; add others as you need them.

INSTALLING KNIVES

The knives slip into the slots in the head and are secured with screws, but the method of installation may be particular to the head design, so be certain to follow the manufacturer's advice for

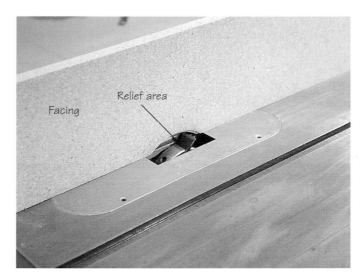

1 An auxiliary wood fence is securely attached to the saw's rip fence. Make the facing as long as the fence and several inches higher if needed for the type of moulding you'll be running, or if the stock will be run on edge.

Facing   Relief area

2 A featherboard, clamped to bear down on the work in front of the cutter, will help keep the work in the correct position.

the correct way to go. In any case, be sure the slots and knives are clean.

Unplug the saw before placing the moulding head on the arbor. Hand-turn the tool after tightening the lock-nut to be sure the knives have clearance through the insert. Stand aside when turning on the machine and then recheck the knives before starting to work.

RIP-FENCE FACING

Most moulding operations, especially those that use only part of a knife's profile, are done by using the rip fence for guidance. This makes it necessary to provide an auxiliary fence, or "facing," of ¾" or 1" stock (photo 1).

To make the relief area, equip the moulding head with blank knives and lower the head so the knives are below the table's surface. Lock the rip fence in position so the facing will receive a cut that is about three-quarters its thickness. Slowly raise the moulding head until the relief arc is about ¾" high.

AT WORK

Moulding heads are asked to work much harder than, say, saw blades, or even dadoing tools, so move the stock across the knives at a slower rate than normal to allow the knives to cut efficiently. Forcing is poor practice and usually results in poor cuts and burn marks on the work and the knives. If

EXAMPLES OF MOULDING KNIVES

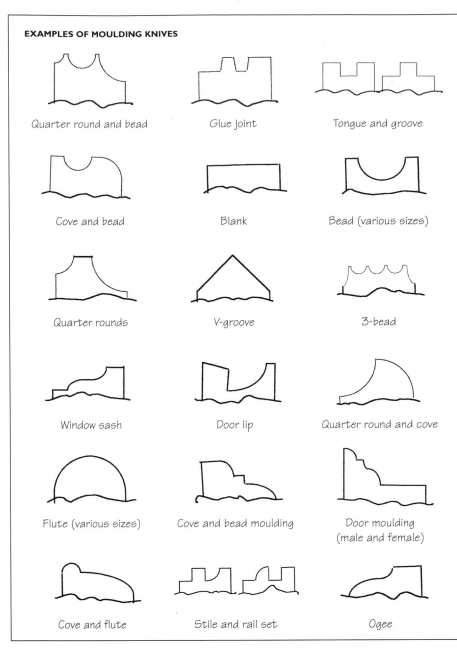

Quarter round and bead

Glue joint

Tongue and groove

Cove and bead

Blank

Bead (various sizes)

Quarter rounds

V-groove

3-bead

Window sash

Door lip

Quarter round and cove

Flute (various sizes)

Cove and bead moulding

Door moulding (male and female)

Cove and flute

Stile and rail set

Ogee

SETUP FOR SLIM MOULDINGS

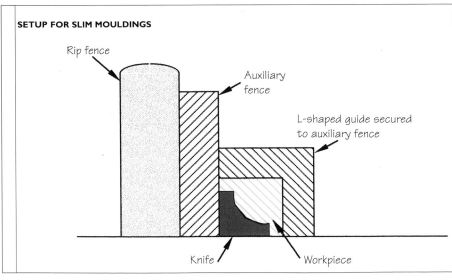

Rip fence

Auxiliary fence

L-shaped guide secured to auxiliary fence

Knife

Workpiece

you feel excessive resistance, it's probably time to think about getting to the full depth of your cut by making repeated passes, raising the head enough each time so the work moves smoothly over the knives.

Keep the work flat on the table and snug against the fence throughout the pass. The depth of the cut is determined by the height of the knives above the table; the width of cut by the position of the fence. Use a featherboard to provide a good hold-down assist (photo 2). As usual in woodworking, cuts are smoothest when made with the grain. When you can't do this, feed the work slowly and make repeated passes to avoid tear-out.

Always make end cuts, especially when the stock is narrow, by using the miter gauge to advance the work (photo 3). Tear-out is inevitable on any shaping cut on end grain at the end of the cut, so do the shaping on a piece that's a bit wider than you need. The imperfection can be removed with a rip cut, making a pass on a jointer or with a hand plane. Make the end cuts first when shaping adjacent edges or all four edges of a piece of work. The final with-the-grain passes will remove the imperfections.

Shaping can also be done with the stock on edge. Be sure to keep the work flat against the fence throughout the pass. Allowing the work to tilt at any time will mar its edges.

SLIM MOULDINGS

A common method of producing slim mouldings is to form the shape on the edge of stock that is wide enough for safe handling and then rip off the milled piece. The procedure can be repeated to supply any number of mouldings, but it can be time-consuming and requires repeated changing from moulding head to saw blade. A more productive method is suggested in the drawing.

Start the job by ripping enough stock to the size of the moulding that's needed. Make the setup so that the L-shaped guide will provide a snug fit for the parent pieces. They should pass

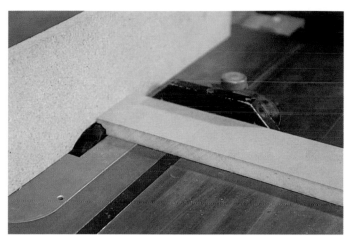

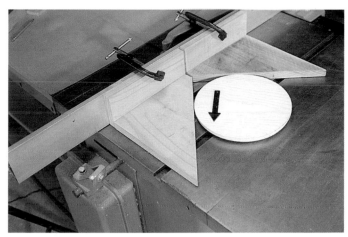

3 End cuts, especially when the work is narrow, are done safely by moving the work with the miter gauge. Be sure of correct alignment. The angle between miter gauge and facing must be 90°.

4 A V-block is used to shape edges of circular components. The units, spaced to accommodate the diameter of the work, are clamped to the rip fence. Brace the work against the right unit and move it forward slowly until it contacts the knives and seats firmly in the V. Rotate the work in a counterclockwise direction.

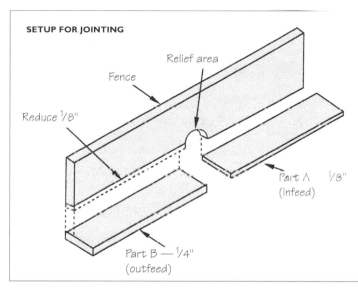

SETUP FOR JOINTING

Fence

Relief area

Reduce 1/8"

Part A   1/8"
(infeed)

Part B — 1/4"
(outfeed)

Jointing, with the head equipped with blank knives, is possible by using the setup shown here. Because the knives are 1" wide, the thickness of stock for the application cannot be more than 7/8".

through the guide without chatter. Start the shaping by feeding the stock into the front end of the setup and end it by pulling it from the rear.

CIRCULAR WORK

Using a moulding head to shape the perimeter of circular components is a feasible application for the moulding cutterhead. What you need is a V-shaped guide that's composed of left- and right-hand parts. The parts are clamped to the fence and are placed so the center line of the V is in line with the center of the moulding head (photo 4).

Start the shaping by bracing the work firmly against the right leg of the V and swinging it slowly until it is

firmly seated. Then slowly rotate the work in a counterclockwise direction. The work must be round and have smooth edges or results will be less than perfect. Be sure the shape you are forming leaves enough edge on the work and guides. To help keep the work flat on the table you can nail a strip of wood across the V to serve as a hold-down.

A SETUP FOR JOINTING

If you don't have a jointer you can use the moulding head, equipped with blank knives, to smooth edges on stock that isn't more than ⅞" thick. What's needed is a setup like the one sketched in the drawing above. As shown, the arrangement is for a ⅛" depth of cut. If

you want less, the thickness of the infeed and outfeed parts and the reduction in the outfeed part of the fence can be adjusted accordingly. Allow the gap at the relief area to be a minimum, just enough for the moulding head knives to spin without a hindrance. An important adjustment — as on a regular jointer — is that the topmost part of the knife's cutting circle be on the same plane as the surface of the outfeed component.

The workpiece, moving forward from the infeed area, should pass smoothly over the cutter and onto the outfeed plate.

It's All in the Box

Learn the tricks to making modular furniture.

Ahouse is a box containing boxes called "rooms," and boxes within those boxes called "furniture." In each area the box is transformed to something useful, beautiful or both. The house-shaped box is architecturally designed to suit a period or personal notions. A furniture-shaped box has legs and drawers and a shaped top to become, for example, a dresser.

In its simplest form, a box is a spartan concept. But to Plato, who used a simple table as a way to discuss truth and the issues of arts and crafts, the idea of a box, like a table, is a "divine truth." There is the idea of the box, there is the builder, and beyond that there might be an artist who doesn't know screws from nails but who can produce an acceptable painting of the project.

But, enough of Plato. Here, the point is that if you accept a box as a piece of furniture, then it is a piece of furniture. I read some time ago about a couple who carried the idea to extreme. Their spacious home was furnished with nothing but boxes, boxes to sit on, platforms to lounge on, others to display artifacts or plants or as storage units. If you visited, you sat on a box and ate off one, and you walked from room to room around modules that served as dividers.

All the boxes were plywood and painted white; color was provided with cushions and pads, wall hangings and rugs. The effect was spectacular, but what I found interesting was that the boxes were "architecturally designed" and put together by commercial cabinetmakers. The professional design fees must have far outweighed material costs. This made me think that a box, or boxes, while simple in construction, can evolve as interesting contributions to a home's decor.

MAKING A BOX

Plywood is a logical material choice. (Use softwood types of plywood for a painted finish, hardwood varieties for a natural look.) Other man-made sheet material is also suitable. Medium Density Fiberboard (MDF) is a good choice for painting because even sawed and sanded edges are easily covered. However, the weight of the material may be a deterrent. Plain old solid lumber might be desirable in some cases, but it's best to use it when project components are narrow enough to avoid having to construct wide panels by edge-gluing separate boards.

You can be persnickety with joint selection or opt for faster production. The lowly butt joint, with nail or screw reinforcement, is usable on lumber or plywood. The problem of exposed plywood edges is solved with self-adhesive banding or by careful filling and sealing. They can also be prepared so they are easy to cover with paint. Miter joints are suitable for any material and can be

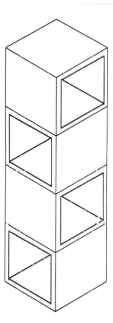

Stack and alternate these boxes to create interesting pedestal storage.

reinforced with splines or biscuits.

Large boxes, like a platform for a mattress or lounge pad, can be strengthened with interior glue blocks. Use plywood for shelves or the slabs needed for desks or tabletops. Cover the edges with slim strips of lumber, glued and nailed. Set the nails and conceal them with wood dough before painting.

MODULAR UNITS

Modular units can be assembled to suit a particular purpose, space or decor. A major advantage of the concept is that you are free at any time to rearrange the units to accommodate changes in

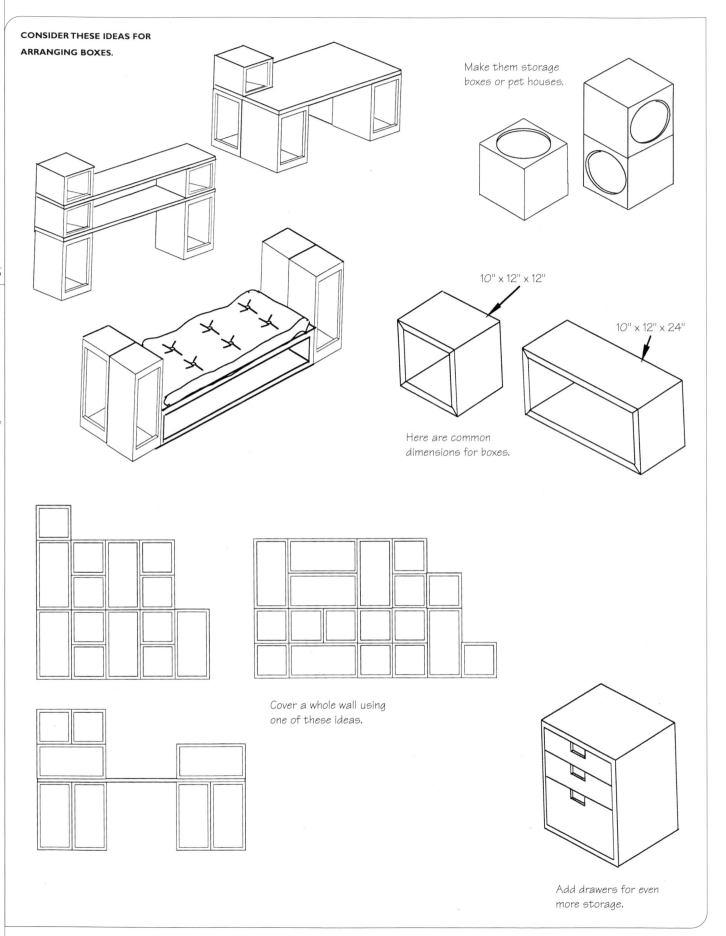

Make them storage boxes or pet houses.

10" x 12" x 12"

10" x 12" x 24"

Here are common dimensions for boxes.

Cover a whole wall using one of these ideas.

Add drawers for even more storage.

FOUR BOXES AND A SHEET OF PLYWOOD MAKE FLEXIBLE SEATING.

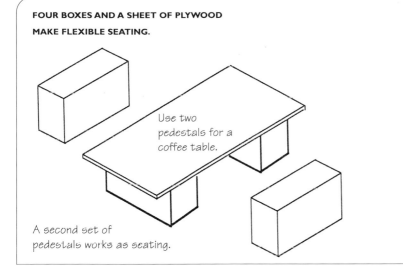

Use two pedestals for a coffee table.

A second set of pedestals works as seating.

TWO OR FOUR PEDESTALS MAKE A DINING TABLE.

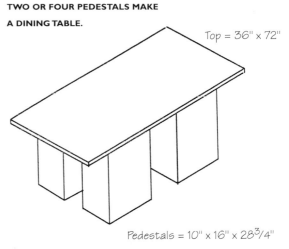

Top = 36" x 72"

Pedestals = 10" x 16" x 28³/4"

THESE ILLUSTRATIONS SHOW THE BASIC JOINTS FOR BASIC BOXES.

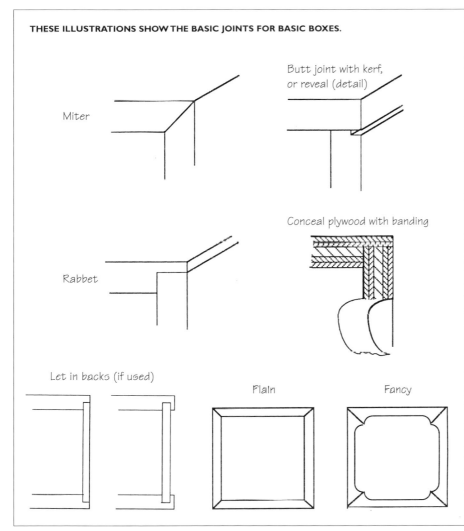

Miter

Butt joint with kerf, or reveal (detail)

Conceal plywood with banding

Rabbet

Let in backs (if used)

Plain   Fancy

storage or display items or merely to provide a change of scene.

Two units, made in quantity, make up a modular project. The units can be sized to suit so long as one of them is half the length of the other. Don't be fazed by the work or time involved; an easy approach is the way to go. The first phase is to cut all the parts to size. Do assembly in stages, producing several at a time. "Suddenly," you'll have enough to cover a wall or to use as a partition.

BE IMAGINATIVE

One project, made by a fellow woodworker, is the combo table shown in the drawing above. Two of the pedestals (boxes) are used to create a coffee table. Guests can be seated on floor-level cushions or on the remaining two boxes. Or, when they are set vertically, the pedestals are sized to provide a suitable height for a dining table.

My friend also has large cubes with one circular opening. Pets enjoy the projects for sleeping or as a hideaway since the interior is lined with carpeting.

Try painting the inside of units with a contrasting color. Install crossing dividers in some units so they are usable to hold bottles of wine.

Combine creativity and practicality when previewing how the final project will appear. So when you hear management gurus tell you to think "outside the box," remember instead to simply think "about the box."

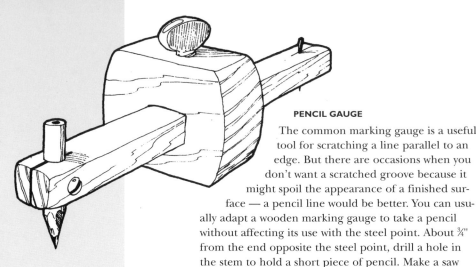

tricks *of the* TRADE

PENCIL GAUGE

The common marking gauge is a useful tool for scratching a line parallel to an edge. But there are occasions when you don't want a scratched groove because it might spoil the appearance of a finished surface — a pencil line would be better. You can usually adapt a wooden marking gauge to take a pencil without affecting its use with the steel point. About ¾" from the end opposite the steel point, drill a hole in the stem to hold a short piece of pencil. Make a saw cut from the end through the hole and about ¼" beyond it. Drill and countersink through the cut between the pencil hole and the stem end for a No. 44 round-head screw to squeeze and grip the pencil.

Percy W. Blandford, Stratford-upon-Avon, England

MY ULTIMATE PUSH STICK

After many years of using different types of table saw push sticks, I've settled on one particular design as the safest and most comfortable. This design puts pressure at the notch and the forward end to hold the stock down while pushing it past the blade. This is especially helpful on thin stock. The shape of the push stick allows me to guide it along the rip fence and rest my hand on the fence, applying pressure as necessary. Thus, if something unexpected were to happen, my hand would not fall or be carried into the blade. I make them out of ¼", ⅜" and ½" plywood scraps. The ¼" works very well when ripping extremely narrow stock.

Robert Colpetzer, Clinton, Tennessee

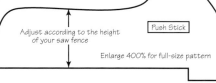

Adjust according to the height of your saw fence

Push Stick

Enlarge 400% for full-size pattern

FINISH CAN RIM GUARD

This simple can guard makes cleaning up the rim and side of my varnish and paint cans unnecessary. It also solves the problem of can lids that fail to seal because of hardened residue left in the rim. To make two rim guards (one for varnish and one for paint), cut three 5"-diameter discs from ⅛" tempered hardboard. On one of the discs, lay out a 4¼"-diameter circle. Cut it out and discard it, keeping the outside ring. From this ring, cut eight segments. On the second and third discs, lay out a 3"-diameter circle and draw a chord (a line from one side of the circle to the other) about 1" from the center point. After cutting out the semicircle and chord on each disc, center each disc on a quart can. Glue the eight ring segments to the bottom of each disc (four on each). Space them equally around the disc and snugly against the can. You now have guards that enable you to strike your brush while keeping the rim and outside free of finish. To make guards for gallon containers, simply increase the dimensions.

Robert Colpetzer, Clinton, Tennessee

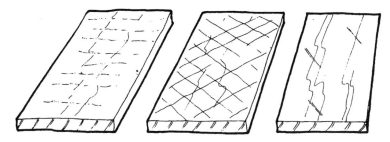

ELIMINATING SANDING DIPS

I build many projects using wide panels of glued-up cedar 1×6s, and used to have difficulty detecting and eliminating dips left by my belt sander. Here's one solution: After initial cross-grain coarse sanding, draw heavy diagonal lines across the surface with a large, soft-lead pencil. Then sand evenly until all the lines are gone. Repeat the procedure, but draw lighter lines as the paper grit gets finer.

C.A. Conway, Benton City, Washington

PAINTING STILTS

Many small projects require finishing on opposite sides, as well as along edges. You have to finish one side, let it dry, then finish the other. Speed up the work with painting stilts. After finishing one side of the project, set it on the stilts and finish the remaining surfaces. Leave it on the stilts if you want to add more coats. When dry, lift the project off and there will be just three small prick marks on the back. Make the stilts by cutting a small triangle, square or circle of ⅜" plywood and driving three or four 6d finishing nails all the way through. It helps to sharpen the nails first on a belt sander or grinder — the sharper the point, the smaller the mark it will leave on the back of the project.

David F. Black, Barnwell, South Carolina

SAVE THAT OLD ANTENNA

Before junking that old radio or television, remove and save the antenna. Those with a telescoping design will provide several diameters, and they're easily cut to different lengths with a tubing cutter for use in shop projects. I've used them as bushings or sleeves in whirligigs and children's toys.

John Tomlin, Niles, Ohio

DOWELING PLYWOOD DRAWERS

When you make drawers out of plywood, screws or nails may not hold very well if they end up positioned in the seam between two of the plys. Try using dowels instead. First cut all the drawer pieces and dry fit them; then glue and clamp them together. After the glue has dried, unclamp the drawer and drill holes in the side pieces where they meet the front and back. Apply glue to lengths of dowel and insert them in the holes.

Dan Labzentis, Endicott, New York

CLAMPING ON AN ANGLE

When clamping on an angle, such as when regluing a splayed chair leg, the clamp has a tendency to slip. A piece of old sandpaper doubled over (rough sides out) and placed under the protecting block will usually provide enough friction to keep the clamp in place.

William P. Nichols,
Ravenna, Ohio

CHUCK KEY WITH LEVERAGE

The best handle for a chuck key not only keeps it handy but provides you with some leverage. Cut off the rounded tip from a discarded broom handle so you have a piece 4" to 6" long. Drill a hole in the flat end slightly smaller than the drill chuck key, and force fit it into the wooden handle with some epoxy for extra grip. Then fit the tip of the rounded end with a screw eye large enough to surround the drill's cord. Open the eye with pliers, slip it around the cord and close it up again. The extra length of your new handle will make loosening tightly chucked bits a breeze.

Don Kinnaman,
Phoenix, Arizona

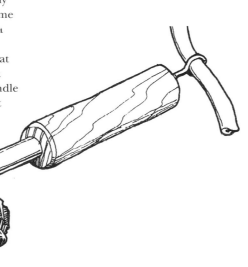

SHELF WITH AN EDGE

If you're having trouble with screwdrivers and other rounded objects rolling off the metal shelf units in your shop, try turning the shelves upside down. Just take the units apart and put them back together. When the shelves are upside down, the 1" edge stands up and provides a barrier — no more looking for things that have fallen behind the shelves.

Beverly L. Puterbaugh,
Piqua, Ohio

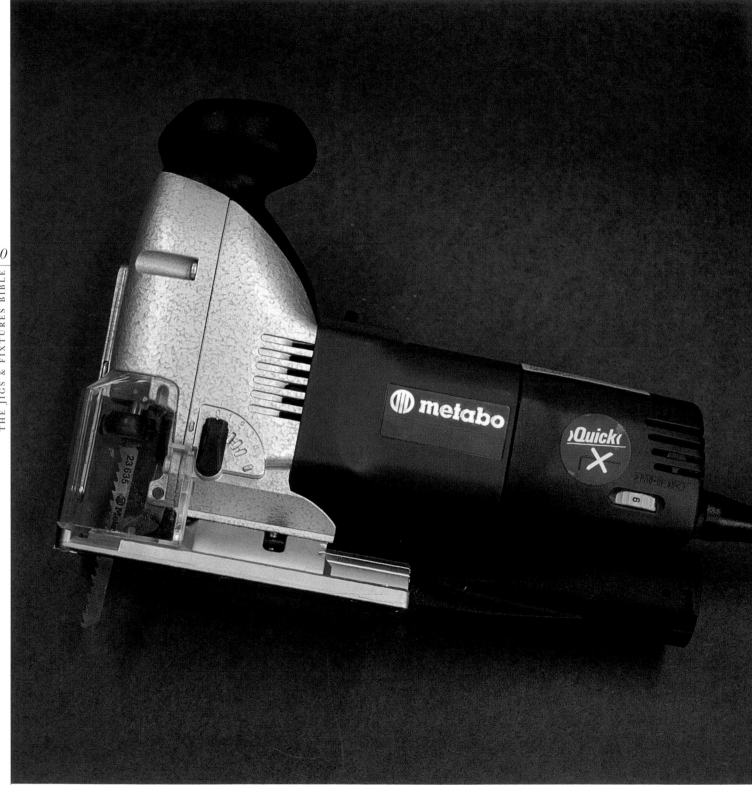

The saber saw's fairly tight radius of turn makes it a highly maneuverable alternative to the band saw, and a fair competitor for much scroll saw work.

The Power Curve Cutters

Saber saw, scroll saw or band saw —

which tool is best for the job?

When workshop curve-cutting chores call for more than a coping saw or keyhole saw, it's time to consider a saber saw, scroll saw or band saw. But which one? All three power tools are proven curve cutters, and there is considerable overlap in function, but each has features that make it particularly well suited for specific woodworking tasks. Whatever the project, one of the saws will be best for the job.

A point about nomenclature — saber saws (sometimes "sabre" saws) may be listed as "jigsaws," and what were once called "jigsaws" are now known as "scroll saws." The tool that hasn't had a name change is the band saw.

THE SABER SAW

Among the curve cutters, the saber saw is the only handheld unit. Its small size and portability are its major advantages. When first introduced, they were touted as portable jigsaws. While a quality saber saw can rival the stationary tools in some areas, it's not a substitute. For starters, blades are secured at one end only, so even the smallest blade must be strong enough to provide rigidity. That fact places some limits on maneuverability. For example,

the blades can't get around tight radii. For the same reason, kerfs are wider, and tooth set doesn't promote the smoothest cuts, although sawing with available hollow-ground blades can improve results considerably.

An exclusive of the saber saw is plunge cutting, a technique that allows one to make internal cutouts without a starting hole for the blade. Hold the tool with the weight resting only on the front edge of the base plate and the blade almost parallel to the board. Turn the saw on and arch the blade slowly and steadily so the blade pierces the work. The procedure can be adopted anywhere — in the center of an 8' panel or through a wall or a fence. Often, plunge cutting is the only way to accomplish a cutout, but in my shop I use a starting hole whenever possible, especially if I can incorporate the arc of the hole as a corner of the cutout.

Advances in saber saw design include orbital sawing action, variable speeds, sawdust blower, adjustable base plate for bevel sawing, and more. Blade stroke ranges from ⅜" to 1" depending on the model. Average blade length is 3½ ", but some units can handle blades as long as 6". With the proper blade, the tool can saw ferrous and nonferrous metals, and there are even knife-edge blades for slicing through linoleum, rubber or leather.

Major accessories include a rip guide for sawing parallel to an edge, and a table to mount the saw in an inverted position so it can be used somewhat as a scroll saw.

THE SCROLL SAW

Scroll saws operate with blank-end blades that are tensioned between upper and lower chucks. The tool can function with blades that are almost hairlike in cross section — so fine you must run a finger lightly along the teeth or view them through a magnifying glass to discover in which direction they are pointing.

No other power tool rivals its smooth cut, the fineness of its kerfs, or its capability in applications such as inlay and marquetry. Therefore, people often think scroll saws are "craft" tools. This view is accurate, but unfair. Modern scroll saws are rugged, variable-speed machines that can function with blades as wide as ¼" and can saw material as thick as 2". Thus, a realistic view is that the tool is practical for general woodworking applications, including techniques such as, say, pad sawing six or eight layers of ¼" plywood to produce duplicate parts or making curved components for furniture, even small cabriole legs.

To make internal cutouts, you must supply an entry hole. The blade, gripped in the lower chuck, is passed through the hole before being secured in the upper chuck. This is also done when using the intriguing "bevel sawing" technique. The idea is to tilt the table to not more than 5°, then cut a series of concentric rings, always keeping the work on the same side of the blade. Each ring, when assembled, will jam into its neighbor so that you create a bowl shape from a flat board. Many workers prepare stock this way for lathe turning. It makes maximum use of a small piece of wood, which is especially gratifying when the material is exotic and expensive.

Scroll saw blades are identified by physical dimensions — thickness, width and teeth per inch (tpi). Many suppliers now use identification numbers (generic), and each number refers to a blade of particular physical makeup. In addition to a variety of blades for wood cutting, there are those especially made for nonwood materials, such as metals, leather, paper and plastics. Actually, there will be a suitable blade for almost anything you wish to cut.

THE BAND SAW

If you ever visit a lumber mill you might see a two-story-high "band mill" sawing logs into boards. These gargantuan machines can work with blades 12" wide and easily slice through green wood. Home-shop band saws have a similar character, but on a smaller scale. Average depth of cut runs 6" to 7"; blade widths start at ⅛" and progress to ½", sometimes ¾".

Like the scroll saw, band saws are often judged by an outstanding application — in this case, compound sawing, the technique used to produce furniture components such as the cabriole leg. The procedure starts by drawing the project's pattern on two adjacent sides of the stock. After one side is cut, the waste pieces are returned to their original positions (with tape or by nailing in waste areas) and the second side is cut. The shape of the piece is revealed when all the waste is removed. I like to think this is something like the sculptor who envisions the form that is within a block of mar-

curve cutters — how they rate

CHORE	SABER SAW	SCROLL SAW	BAND SAW
pad sawing	limited	limited	best
piercing internal cuts	good	good	
plunge cuts	good		
resawing		limited	best
halving rounds		limited	best
crosscutting	good	slow	best
ripping	good	slow	best
location work	best		
curve cutting (general)	good	good	best
curve cutting (intricate)	limited	best	limited
fretwork		excellent	
in-the-field	best		
cut depth	limited	limited	excellent
cut speed	good (variable)	good (variable)	fastest
compound cutting		limited	best
sanding		*	*
guided circular cuts	most flexible	good	good
filing		possible	
internal bevel sawing	possible	best	
rip cut capacity	unlimited	good**	limited
bevel sawing	good	good	good
inlay		best	
metal cutting	good	good	best***
precutting for lathe work		limited	good
forming slots	good	good	
smooth cuts	good****	best	limited*****

Key

* — *Limited ability, with accessory if available*

** — *Better ability here if arm can be removed or swung down*

*** — *Best if with variable-speed or geared-speed control*

**** — *Good if used with hollow-ground blade*

***** — *Will always have "washboarding" that requires some amount of sanding*

ble. Compound sawing is also a practical way to prepare stock for lathe turning since it's a fast way to remove material you would otherwise have to cut away with chisels.

"Resawing" is another band saw exclusive. You can cut a thick board into a number of thinner pieces, but there's more to it. For example: If I need a number of identical shelf brackets, I would saw the shape in a block of, say, 4" × 4", and then resaw the block into the number of parts I want. Pad sawing is another way to pro-

duce multiple similar parts. On a typical band saw you can, for example, pad saw 24 pieces of ¼" plywood or 12 pieces of ½" stock!

For curve cutting, the tool rivals the saber saw, but it has a width-of-cut limitation (the distance from the blade to the arm support) so it isn't as flexible. And the tool can't compete with a scroll saw for intricate curve cutting, though with a ⅛" blade, it can make some fairly tight turns. Internal cutouts are not possible since the blade is a continuous loop. However, extremists don't hesitate to break the blade so it can be passed through a starting hole and then weld it together again for the sawing.

Guided rip or crosscuts are practical so long as the blade is sharp and in prime condition. When the blade "leads" — that is, moves off the cut line to the left or right — it's usually caused by tooth damage or incorrectly set teeth, and should be replaced or reconditioned. Some modern band saws provide variable speed or have a gear mechanism for speed reduction so with the correct blade, the tool can cut nonwood materials such as ferrous and nonferrous metals.

MAKING THE CHOICE

For "housework," such as remodeling, installing an extra window or a skylight, or installing paneling, a saber saw offers great features. It's also good for outside work such as erecting fences and screens.

If furniture, whether modern or traditional, was my major interest, a band saw would be my first choice.

If I were in my shop mostly for fun, wanted to introduce a youngster to woodworking or wanted to establish a cottage industry producing toys and small projects, a scroll saw would be the tool of choice.

The conventional 10" band saw found in small shops has a 6" to 7" depth of cut and can resaw lumber and cut tight circles using a ⅛"-wide blade. For furniture making, it offers the most versatility of the curve-cutting saws.

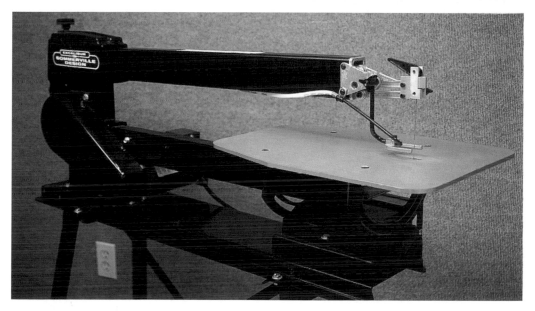

The scroll saw can use blank-end or pin-end blades and has a variable-speed control. Usually, the table tilts for bevel sawing.

A Plane Miracle

Plane rough lumber and make miles of moulding with one machine.

One of the most intriguing experiences in woodworking is watching a rough board emerge from a thickness planer. Magically, the true character of the wood's surface is revealed (photo 1). The same can be said for seeing a piece of rectangular stock emerge as an intricate moulding profile.

There was a time when home-shop woodworkers who needed to smooth a number of boards would truck them to a local lumberyard where an employee ran them through a monster machine for a fee — negating the bargain of buying lumber in the rough. We yearned for the day we would be able to transform rough lumber into finished stock in our own shops. And the concept of making our own moulding simply was unthinkable.

Now those dreams are a reality because of the fairly recent introduction of "small" units that can be purchased for less than $1,000. And other planer/moulders, such as the Jet, can be used to make moulding by the yard or the mile. While the machine doesn't look like the machines in the mills, it is structurally similar and is ample for the home and small commercial shop. The Jet can accommodate 13"-wide boards up to 6⅛" thickness. The 1½-hp motor rotates the three-knife cutterhead at 4,500 rpms, which provides 13,500 cuts per minute. There are two

automatic feed rates: 20 feet per minute for planing and 10 feet per minute for moulding cuts.

Operating this machine doesn't require expertise, but there are essential rules to follow to ensure quality results.

PLANING

Planing refers to smoothing a board or reducing its thickness while producing a plane that is parallel to the opposite surface. The board is moved smoothly into the infeed end of the machine until it is gripped by a feed roller that automatically moves it past the cutterhead where a second roller helps move the work and keep it flat on the planer bed. Always feed stock so the knives are shaving with the grain of the wood. Grain direction might not be obvious when working with rough wood, but you can usually determine it by making a slight rip cut along the edge of the board.

All thickness planers have limits to the depth they can cut. On the Jet, a ⅛" cut is allowable on stock that is narrower than 5½", but 1/16" is the maximum cut on wider stock. In all cases, you get the best results by making a few light cuts rather than a single heavy one. Your board must not be shorter than 14" or less than ½" thick. I'll talk a little later about ways to get around these restrictions.

Keeping the board flat throughout the pass is very important. "Snipe" — a thickness planer bugaboo that is actually a slight depression on either end of a planed board — is usually caused by failing to support the work on a true plane throughout the pass. Snipe can occur, for example, when the weight of a board entering or leaving the planer tilts the board up into the cutterhead so more wood is removed at the end of the pass. That's one reason extending the length of your planer bed is a must.

Accessory extension tables are available, as are freestanding roller stands. I made my own extension table (diagram 1). If you duplicate this, have the steel bars bolted in position and secure a long board on the planer bed by raising the table so the feed rollers grip the board. Clamp the extension to the board before installing the self-tapping screws. Lock each extension with four bolts. If you remove one bolt from each side and loosen the others, the extensions can fold down for storage (photo 2).

You need a "bedboard" that's secured to the planer bed for moulding operations. If you design it like the one shown in diagram 2, it also will serve as a base for attaching jigs that add convenience and accuracy to particular operations. One jig, shown in photo 3, ensures the boards will be held vertically when doing edge-planing or jointing. This also is the setup to use when using moulding knives to form glue joints or tongue-and-groove joints. The reason for not gluing the upright — or fence — to the jig's base (see diagram 3) is so you can supply a fence of a different height if you need one.

MOULDING

Moulding knives are available in shapes ranging from quarter-round to crown moulding. Large ones are installed in place of the planer knives, but ones that are 2" or less in width can be used without removing the planer knives in

1 It's "hands off" as soon as the work makes contact with the infeed roller. The machine takes over, moving the work from start to finish. It's important that the tool be equipped with extension tables both fore and aft to avoid planer troubles such as "snipe."

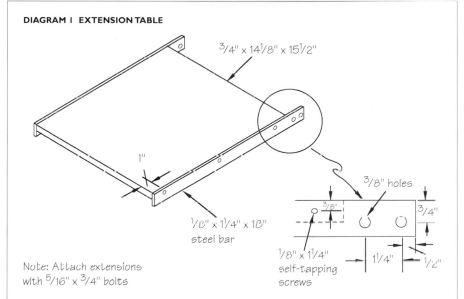

DIAGRAM 1 EXTENSION TABLE

¾" x 14⅛" x 15½"

1"

⅛" x 1¼" x 18" steel bar

Note: Attach extensions with 5/16" x ¾" bolts

3/8" holes

3/8"

3/4"

⅛" x 1¼" self-tapping screws

1¼"

½"

the Jet. The moulding knives, in sets of three, must be aligned in the cutterhead. To ensure this, a gauge, which is shown in photo 4, is furnished. With one knife in place, the others are installed so they barely touch the gauge when the cutterhead is turned by hand. Incidentally, this is one area of woodworking where you should wear tight-fitting gloves. Planer and moulding knives are sharp.

Wood to be moulded must be aligned with the knives and guided in a straight line throughout the pass. One way to ensure this is to form a tunnel by clamping parallel strips of wood to the bedboard. A better way is to make an adjustable jig that will accommodate different widths (see photo 5 and diagram 4). In some

cases, depending on the size and style of the knives, the feed rollers have to be lowered. Because this is covered in the manuals, there's little point in repeating it here.

It's always a good idea, especially when working with a new knife setup, to make a trial cut on scrap material. And, as always, you get better results by making several light cuts.

CURVED MOULDING

It might seem strange to think you can produce curved moulding with a planer, yet it's a practical application. The possible radius of the curve depends somewhat on the size of the machine, but you'll find that smaller radii are more limited than large. The procedure is fairly simple but calls for a pre-

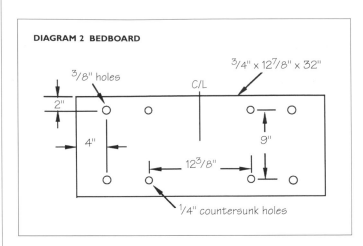

DIAGRAM 2 BEDBOARD

3/8" holes

2"

C/L

3/4" x 12⅞" x 32"

4"

9"

12⅜"

¼" countersunk holes

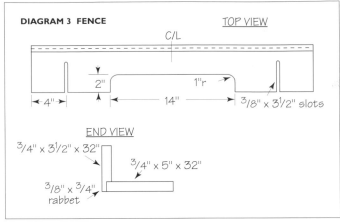

DIAGRAM 3 FENCE

TOP VIEW

C/L

2"

1"r

4"

14"

3/8" x 3½" slots

END VIEW

3/4" x 3½" x 32"

3/4" x 5" x 32"

3/8" x 3/4" rabbet

moulder/planers at a glance

COMPANY	JET	SEARS	RBI	WOODMASTER	WILLIAMS & HUSSEY	BELSAW
Model #	JPM-13	23383N	812	712	W7	985-5
HP	1½	2½*	2	5	2	5
Cutter RPM	4,500	4,500	5,500	4,200	7,000	4,200
Speed (FPM)	10/20	13/26	11	0-16	15	12/20
# of Knives	3	3	2	3	2	3
Width Capacity	13"	12½"	12¼"	12¼"	7"	12⅜"
Thickness Capacity	6⅛"	5"	8"	6¾"	8"	6¼"
Retail Price	$999	$750	$1,599	$1,952 list	$1,968 list	$1,875
Contact #	800-274-6848	800-377-7414	800-487-2623	800-821-6651	800-258-1380	800-468-4449

Developed horsepower

2 The extension tables pivot down to minimize storage space. I made my tables with medium density fiberboard. It's a good idea to seal all edges and surfaces before installing the pieces. Keep them bright and smooth with an occasional application of paste wax.

cise jig setup like the one shown in diagram 5. "Inside" and "outside" guides that suit the exact curve of the work are secured to a base that in turn is clamped to the bedboard so the intersecting center lines of the jig and moulding knives are exactly aligned. This can be established visually by making the setup with the dust hood temporarily removed.

Once you are organized, feed the work through the jig just as you would a piece of straight stock. One thing is certain: If you can't move the work smoothly through the guides by hand, don't expect the machine to do it.

OTHER TECHNIQUES

Boards that are too short to be fed through the planer can be butted end to end with other boards so they can be processed like they were a single piece (diagram 6). A fellow woodworker connects the boards by gluing them — not a joint I would recommend, but

 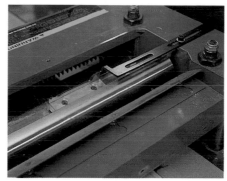 

3 Tall fences keep the work vertical when planing edges and when using moulding knives to form glue joints or tongue-and-groove joints. The jig adjusts to accommodate various stock thicknesses.

4 A gauge is furnished so moulding knives, which come in sets of three, can be correctly aligned. Allow the machine to run down for a few minutes when you're finished, then check all the locking screws.

5 Strips to be moulded must be guided to move straight and in line with the knives. The jig I made is adjustable so it can be used with various stock widths. Be sure the guides are parallel.

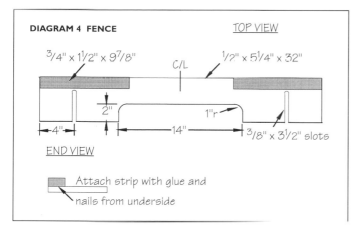

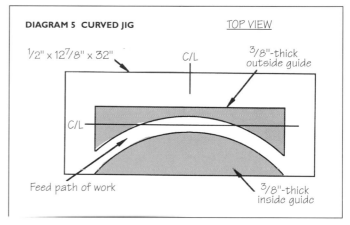

it serves the purpose. After he planes them, he snaps the boards apart or cuts them on the glue line.

Feed rollers flatten warped stock as it goes through the planer, but because of wood's inherent springback, the warp will return when the pass is complete. Narrow thick pieces might resist the temporary flattening, but not wide ones. One way to get around this is to flatten the convex surface on a jointer so you'll have a flat face to put down on the planer bed. Another system involves placing the warped board on a larger flat board, with shims under the warp (diagram 6). This will remove warp, but with considerable loss to the thickness of your wood. So face it, extreme warp cannot be cured. It's better to rip the board into several pieces, each of which can be planed and then reassembled with glue.

To square stock precisely, it's best to smooth two adjacent sides on a jointer and then finish on the planer (dia-

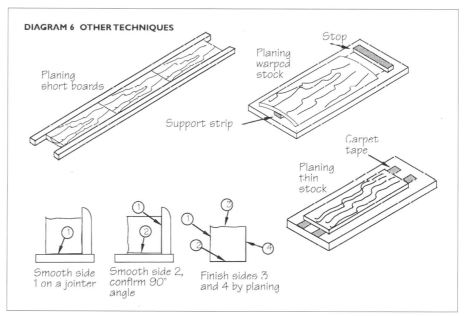

gram 6).

Planing stock thinner than the machine normally allows can be accomplished by securing the work to a thicker board and passing them together through the planer. Carpet tape

has enough bond to keep the pieces together. If you have a lot of these thin boards to plane, it might be worth your while to "veneer" your larger support board with 150-grit (or coarser) sandpaper.

The outboard support (table extension) allows the use of even heavy-duty routers. An access slot in the jig's braces accepts a C-clamp when one is need-ed for additional work security.

Make Miter Joints That Have Teeth

This simple jig allows you to easily cut splines in your miter joints.

Miter joints are classic and practical woodworking connections because they make wood turn a corner while hiding end grain. But while they leave a pleasant-looking joint line, they are lacking in one important way: The glue strength of a miter isn't nearly as strong as a long-grain joint. And since we know these short-grain to short-grain joints aren't strong, it's essential that miter joints be reinforced.

The most practical solution is to cut matching slots into the two mating edges and glue a spline in the slots. Splines keep the components locked together and help prevent separation caused by stresses and changes in atmospheric conditions. You can form the slots with a dadoing tool or by simply making repeat passes with a saw blade. But in the case of a picture frame, you have to make identical cuts into eight edges, so some fussing is required to achieve accuracy. Most woodworkers make miters frequently enough to welcome a convenient and reliable way to form spline slots precisely.

My jig works with a portable router. Straight bits, available in various diameters, do the cutting. A two-edged miter guide allows working on left- or right-hand cuts. The fence can be positioned to accommodate various stock

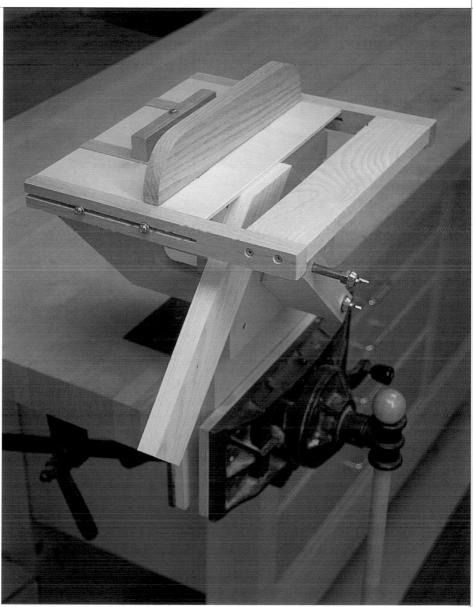

The slotting jig can be clamped in a vise or secured to the edge of a workbench. The jig's clamp swivels so it can be used to secure left- or right-hand miters.

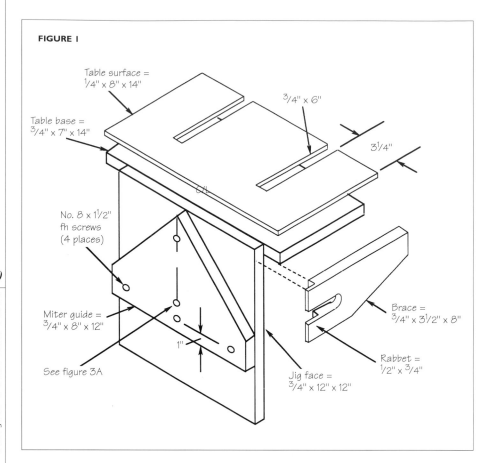

FIGURE 1

Table surface = 1/4" x 8" x 14"

3/4" x 6"

3 1/4"

Table base = 3/4" x 7" x 14"

No. 8 x 1 1/2" fh screws (4 places)

Miter guide = 3/4" x 8" x 12"

1"

See figure 3A

Brace = 3/4" x 3 1/2" x 8"

Rabbet = 1/2" x 3/4"

Jig face = 3/4" x 12" x 12"

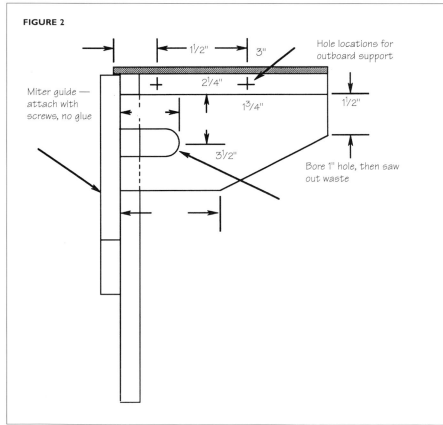

FIGURE 2

1 1/2"

3"

2 1/4"

Hole locations for outboard support

Miter guide — attach with screws, no glue

1 3/4"

1 1/2"

3 1/2"

Bore 1" hole, then saw out waste

thicknesses. The outboard support (table extension) will maintain even the heaviest router on "firm footing."

CONSTRUCTING THE JIG

Construction details for the jig's body are shown in Figures 1 and 2. Start by using ¾" plywood for the jig's face and the table base. Join these parts with glue and 6d finishing nails. The hardwood braces are next. Your best bet is to cut a piece of stock twice as long as you need and to form the rabbet at each end; then shape the round-end slot that provides access for a C-clamp when one is needed. First bore a ¾" hole and then saw out the waste. Now you can halve the part and form the tapers so you end up with two braces. Remember that these are left- and right-hand components.

To add the braces, first coat contact areas with glue, then use finishing nails in the jig's face and two or three No. 8 × 1½" flathead screws down through the table base. Be sure that the angle between the face of the jig and the table base is 90°.

Cut a piece of tempered hardboard to the size of the table surface, then form the slots needed for the fence guides. You can form these slots as you did those in the braces. You can attach the table surface by using glue or contact cement. If you use contact cement, don't coat the areas where the slots will be. In either case, be sure the front edge of the table surface projects ¼" beyond the jig's face.

Cut the piece required for the miter guide, draw an accurate center line across its width and then use a right-angle template to mark the 45° lines. Saw outside the lines and finish to the lines by sanding. Drill and counterbore for the carriage bolt that is needed for the clamp before installing the miter guide (see figure 3A on page 122). The miter guide is held with screws — no glue. This is so it can be replaced or adjusted if necessary. Be sure the angle between the bearing edges of the guide and the projection of the table surface is 45°.

Figure 3 details how the clamp is made. Don't cut the piece to shape

FIGURE 3

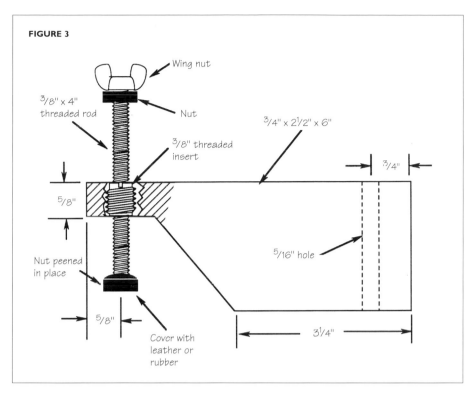

Wing nut

$^3/_8$" x 4" threaded rod

Nut

$^3/_8$" threaded insert

$^3/_4$" x $2^1/_2$" x 6"

$^3/_4$"

$^5/_8$"

$^5/_16$" hole

Nut peened in place

$^5/_8$"

Cover with leather or rubber

$3^1/_4$"

FIGURE 3A

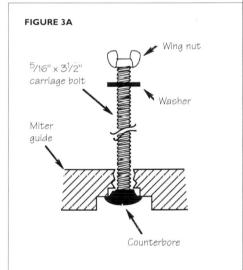

Wing nut

$^5/_16$" x $3^1/_2$" carriage bolt

Washer

Miter guide

Counterbore

FIGURE 4

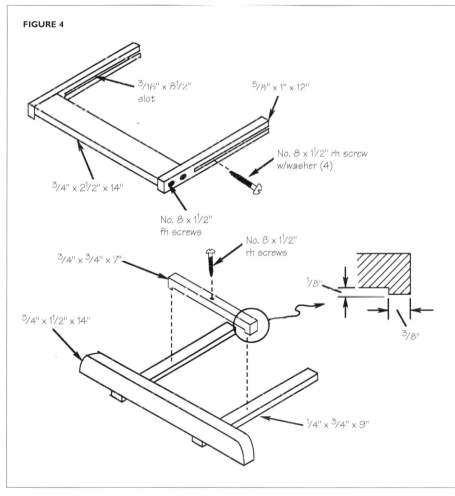

$^3/_16$" x $8^1/_2$" slot

$^5/_8$" x 1" x 12"

No. 8 x $1^1/_2$" rh screw w/washer (4)

$^3/_4$" x $2^1/_2$" x 14"

No. 8 x $1^1/_2$" fh screws

$^3/_4$" x $^3/_4$" x 7"

No. 8 x $1^1/_2$" rh screws

$^1/_8$"

$^3/_4$" x $1^1/_2$" x 14"

$^3/_8$"

$^1/_4$" x $^3/_4$" x 9"

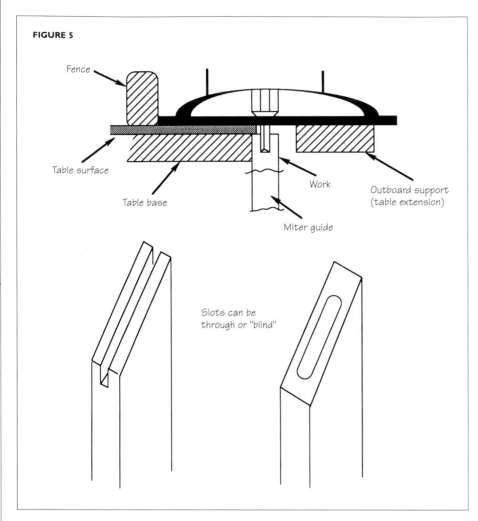

FIGURE 5

Fence

Table surface

Table base

Miter guide

Work

Outboard support
(table extension)

Slots can be
through or "blind"

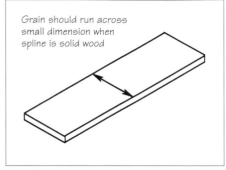

Grain should run across
small dimension when
spline is solid wood

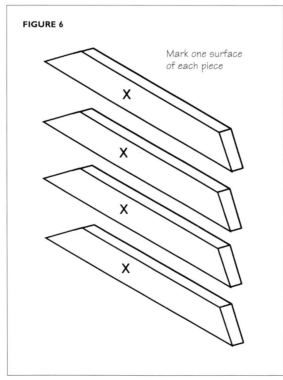

FIGURE 6

Mark one surface
of each piece

X

X

X

X

until after you have installed the threaded insert and drilled the ³⁄₁₆" hole.

Figure 4 supplies construction information for the outboard support and the fence. When you install the screws that secure the support, have the assembly in place so its top edges are flush with the table surface.

USING THE JIG

Place your workpiece against the miter guide and push it up so the miter cut butts against the projection of the table surface. Secure it with the jig's clamp or, whenever necessary, an extra clamp. Adjust the fence so the router bit will be on the center line of the miter cut and move the router left to right (figure 5). As always, when a deep cut is needed, results are better when the chore is accomplished by making repeat passes. When this is necessary, make the initial cut on all parts before changing the projection of the router bit.

Mark the same surface on each of the components (figure 6) and place this surface against the face of the jig. This way the slots will be aligned even if they are not exactly centered.

For light-duty work, the jig can be used with a rotary cutter like the Bosch SpirAcut or Ryobi's Multi-Tool. Be aware though that the penetrating bits normally used with such a tool won't work for this application. You must still work with a regular router bit.

CAUTION

The jig is a most useful accessory but it will not guarantee results if you are careless when sawing the miters.

The cuts must be 45° for results to be perfect.

Another Way To Recycle

Try these clever ways to use the old garden hose in your shop.

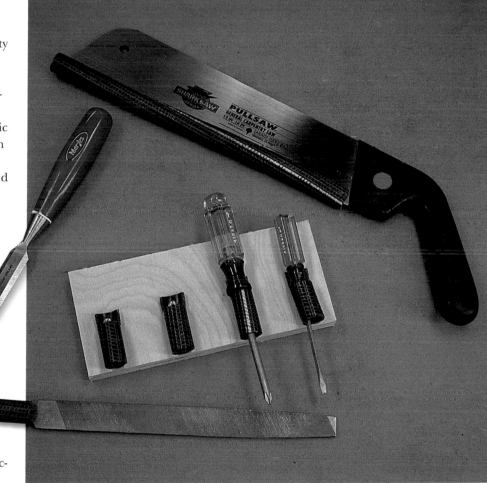

Anyone living in an unpredictable climate, which is pretty much everyone I know, faces the prospect of an electricity outage.

Well, when you live in an all-electric environment, as I most certainly do in my shop, the possible result of rain and high winds is a power outage. And that means no heat, no light, no power, no working in the shop. So during a prolonged electric-less period, I came across a bundle of unsalvageable garden hose and, thinking "shop," as always, I reasoned that recycling the material in shop-wise ways would be a good project.

The thoughts I had are shown on the accompanying pages. I'm sure that *Popular Woodworking* readers will envision many others.

I used a utility knife to separate sections and to form slits or slots. To shape ends for "ties" I used a coping saw with a fine blade. This leaves rough edges that can be smoothed with the knife or with sandpaper.

To make a handle, say, for a file, I filled a suitable length of hose with a product called Durham's Rock Hard Water Putty. The product comes as a powder that can be mixed to various consistencies with water. After filling the hose with putty, I pressed it onto the tang of the file and then left it alone until the putty hardened.

Necessity is not alone the mother of invention. Sometimes, power outages serve the same purpose!

CREATE STORAGE FOR SCREWDRIVERS, CHISELS, AWLS AND OTHER TOOLS.

Make a rack for lathe tools. The hose can have a "tie" at each end that can be used to attach the hose to a piece of wood.

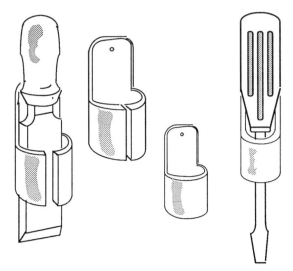

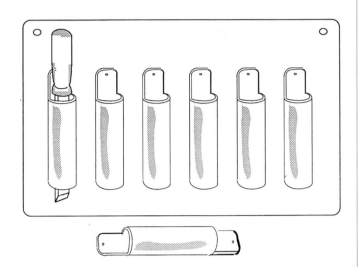

HERE ARE A FEW OTHER WAYS THE HOSE MIGHT BE USED.

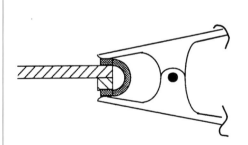

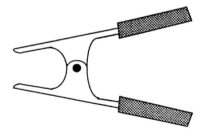

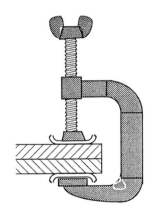

Spring clamp pads protect your work.

Wrap handles of tools.

Use the hose for C-clamp pads.

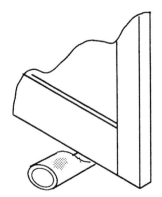

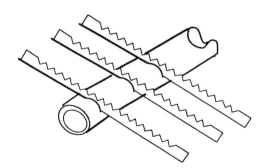

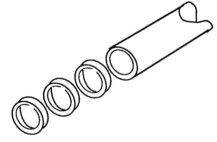

Devise a doorstop.

Slice a holder for scroll saw blades.

Cut rubber washers.

PROTECT YOUR HANDS.

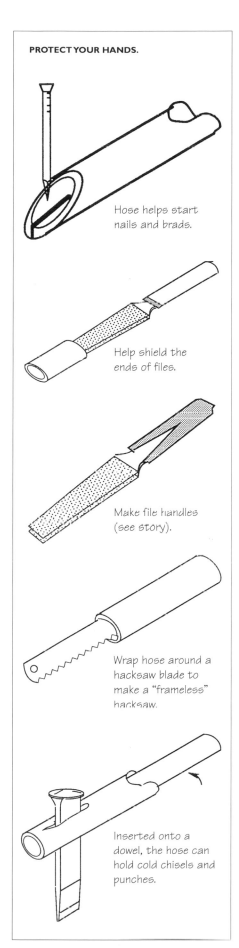

Hose helps start nails and brads.

Help shield the ends of files.

Make file handles (see story).

Wrap hose around a hacksaw blade to make a "frameless" hacksaw.

Inserted onto a dowel, the hose can hold cold chisels and punches.

PROTECT THE CUTTING EDGES OF YOUR TOOLS.

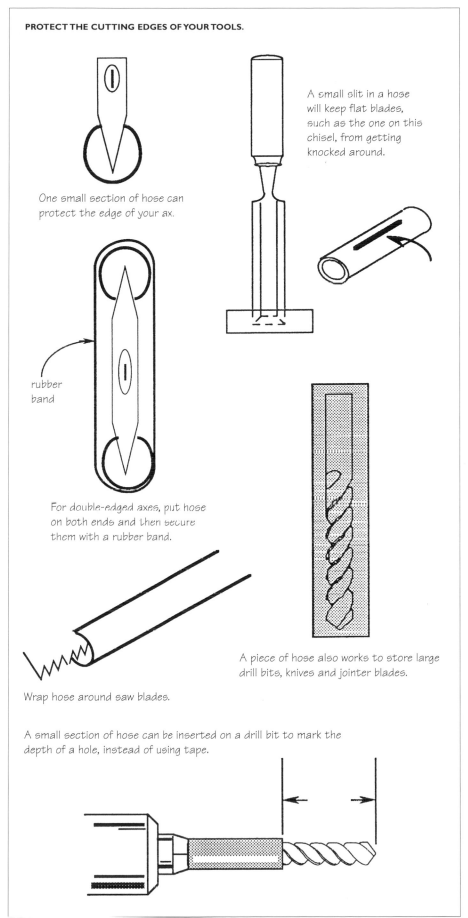

One small section of hose can protect the edge of your ax.

rubber band

For double-edged axes, put hose on both ends and then secure them with a rubber band.

A small slit in a hose will keep flat blades, such as the one on this chisel, from getting knocked around.

A piece of hose also works to store large drill bits, knives and jointer blades.

Wrap hose around saw blades.

A small section of hose can be inserted on a drill bit to mark the depth of a hole, instead of using tape.